In Praise of *A Better Choice*

"Nancy Pelosi famously told us that we could find out what   1.
It is now five years later, and thanks to its convoluted conce
regulations few have wended their way through the ACA, ai
Fortunately John Goodman has studied the Act and has writ   *...hoice*
that reveals what is in the ACA, what is wrong with it, and wh   ... done to provide
cost-effective healthcare to our citizens. The ACA starts from ti   ...se that the federal government
knows best when it comes to the provision of healthcare. John Goodman shows the pitfalls of this
premise and how the market can be harnessed to align consumer choice and provider incentives to more
effectively resolve the issues of resource use and financing of healthcare."

> —**June E. O'Neill**, Wollman Distinguished Professor of Economics and Director of the Center
> for the Study of Business and Government, Baruch College; former Director, Congressional
> Budget Office

"John Goodman understands the real life effects of the Affordable Care Act and the proposed alternatives. John also writes extremely well, making complicated concepts clear. All this makes *A Better
Choice* a highly recommended read for those who wish to understand the current health policy debate."

> —**Bill Cassidy**, M.D., U.S. Senator

"John Goodman has written a clear and compelling analysis of America's health care morass. Anyone
who wants to understand what the politicians and policy wonks are arguing about should turn to *A Better Choice*. Liberals and conservatives should both read this book to understand why Obamacare does
not work as it was supposed to. Everyone should read this book to learn what the solution is."

> —**Joseph R. Antos**, Wilson H. Taylor Scholar in Health Care and
> Retirement Policy, American Enterprise Institute

"Regardless of whether the Affordable Care Act (ACA) has any merit in theory, its practical realities
point toward a death spiral as it will likely collapse under its own weight, for all the reasons Goodman
lucidly recounts in *A Better Choice*. He offers a thoughtful, thought-provoking alternative to the ACA
(Obamacare) and the enormous harms it would cause, to which everyone, especially all those who favor
free markets and limited government, should pay very close attention."

> —**E. Haavi Morreim**, Professor, College of Medicine, Univ. of Tennessee Health Science Center

"One good thing that has come out of the Affordable Care Act is that it has produced serious debate
about how to fix the American healthcare system. An excellent place for readers interested in this question to start would be John C. Goodman's *A Better Choice*, which zeroes in on the many problems with
the ACA and proposes workable, market-based, alternatives."

> —**Joel M. Zinberg**, M.D., J.D., F.A.C.S., Associate Clinical Professor, Icahn School of Medicine
> at Mount Sinai Hospital

"In *A Better Choice*, John Goodman has worked a miracle. He has distilled the essence of a plan to
improve the limping and vulnerable Obamacare program into four points (read the book to find out),
which improve opportunities for choice, improve efficiency in that choice, and expand the set of people
likely to end up with health insurance coverage. Not that everyone on either left or right will agree with
all of the particulars of each point or their suggested implementation—but the book provides a fresh
starting point, an alternative narrative, that is virtually guaranteed to get us to a better place than we are
at present."

> —**Mark V. Pauly**, Bendheim Professor, Professor of Health Care Management, and Professor of
> Business and Public Policy, Wharton School, University of Pennsylvania

"John Goodman achieves something most writers only dream of. His strongest adversaries openly endorse his books as 'must-reads.' In a politically charged atmosphere, his book *Priceless* won praise from across the political spectrum. Now, *A Better Choice* offers serious ideas for pulling American healthcare out of its current morass. You don't have to agree with all or even with most of Goodman's ideas to find *A Better Choice* indispensable."

—**Robert F. Graboyes**, Senior Research Fellow, Mercatus Center, George Mason University

"The Affordable Care Act signed into law by President Obama abruptly altered the pathway of healthcare in the U.S. Contrary to the desire of most Americans, this government centralization was undertaken without understanding, or perhaps even in spite of, the deleterious impact it would have on medical care access, quality, and cost, and without regard for its broader harms to employment and future healthcare innovation. In *A Better Choice*, John Goodman articulates the important problems with Obamacare in clear language, laying out the core impacts of the law for all those interested in truly understanding the issues. He then details how to transition to a healthcare system that provides access to all while maintaining the high quality of what is factually the world's best medical care. I highly recommend the book to all those interested in the future of America's healthcare."

—**Scott W. Atlas**, David and Joan Traitel Senior Fellow, Hoover Institution, Stanford University

"John Goodman has been one of the most important health economists. He has been an informed and prescient critic of the current health system, and his forecasts of the failings of Obamacare have been exactly on target. He has also been a leader in proposing workable alternatives, and his health savings account plan has been a success whenever it has been used. In *A Better Choice* he continues this important work. He first shows in detail what is wrong with Obamacare. But he does not stop there: he provides the important alternative, fixed-sum tax credits, that should replace all other health subsidies, including the subsidy for employer-provided health insurance. He shows how this plan could greatly improve the efficiency of our healthcare system and also lead to increased healthcare for the disadvantaged. This is a serious book and one the new Congress should examine very carefully."

—**Paul H. Rubin**, Samuel Candler Dobbs Professor of Economics, Emory University

"*A Better Choice* is an intriguing book that combines John Goodman's most sensible proposals all in one place. On the one hand it contrasts the Affordable Care Act vision with the reality. On the other hand it outlines how simple a real solution might be."

—**Thomas R. Saving**, Jeff Montgomery Professor of Economics and Director of the Private Enterprise Research Center, Texas A & M University

"After half a decade of turmoil generated by the Affordable Care Act in a three trillion dollar healthcare economy, John Goodman's *A Better Choice* succinctly diagnoses the problems and lays out a practical treatment plan. His six principles of health reform transcend the poison and dishonesty of late and offer the proper terms for a real solution. As politicians search to find remedies before the health economy is too damaged to alter course, they will be well served reading and acting on the policy prescriptions in *A Better Choice*."

—**Stephen T. Parente**, Minnesota Insurance Industry Chair of Health Finance and Director of the Medical Industry Leadership Institute, University of Minnesota

"As Obamacare continues to present us with more complications and disappointments, *A Better Choice* indeed offers in clear and compelling terms, a better choice for all Americans—one that strips away the bureaucratic controls and mandates, and allows consumers to take over their own healthcare decisions. John Goodman provides a devastating indictment of the current system, and supplies a clear roadmap toward a more certain and prosperous future."

—**Richard A. Epstein**, Laurence A. Tisch Professor of Law, New York University

A BETTER CHOICE
HEALTHCARE SOLUTIONS
for AMERICA

JOHN C. GOODMAN

The INDEPENDENT INSTITUTE

Oakland, California

The Independent Institute
100 Swan Way, Oakland, CA 94621-1428
Telephone: 510-632-1366
Fax: 510-568-6040
Email: info@independent.org
Website: www.independent.org

Cover Design: Denise Tsui
Cover Image: Cultura Asia / Rafe Swan / Getty Images

Goodman, John C., author.
  A Better Choice : healthcare solutions for America / by John C.
Goodman.
    p. ; cm.
  Includes bibliographical references.
  ISBN 978-1-59813-208-3 (pbk. : alk. paper)
  I. Goodman, John C. Healthcare solutions for post-Obamacare America.
II. Independent Institute (Oakland, Calif.), issuing body. III. Title.
  [DNLM: 1. United States. Patient Protection and Affordable Care Act.
2. Health Care Reform—United States. 3. Insurance, Health—United States.
W 275 AA1]
  RA771.5
  362.1′0425—dc23   2014048090

Contents

THE INDEPENDENT INSTITUTE is a non-profit, non-partisan, scholarly research and educational organization that sponsors in-depth studies of critical social and economic issues. The mission of the Independent Institute is to boldly advance peaceful, prosperous, and free societies grounded in a commitment to human worth and dignity.

Today, the influence of partisan interests is so pervasive that public-policy debate has become too politicized and is largely confined to a narrow reconsideration of existing policies. In order to fully understand the nature of public issues and possible solutions, the Institute adheres to the highest standards of independent scholarly inquiry.

The resulting studies are published and widely distributed as books, articles in *The Independent Review*, policy reports, working papers, and other publications. Events sponsored by the Institute bring together scholars and policy experts to debate issues and discuss their implications.

Through uncommon independence, depth, and clarity, the Independent Institute expands the frontiers of our knowledge of public policy and fosters new and effective directions for government reform.

100 Swan Way, Oakland, California 94621-1428, U.S.A.
Telephone: 510-632-1366 • Facsimile: 510-568-6040 • Email: info@independent.org • www.independent.org

1

Introduction

BARACK OBAMA FAMOUSLY campaigned during the 2008 election season on a platform of change. Pundits and partisans can debate whether or not his tenure in the Oval Office has lived up to that promise on other fronts. But all agree that President Obama's signature legislative victory, the Patient Protection and Affordable Care Act of 2010 has brought major changes to the American healthcare system.

It's also undeniable that "Obamacare," as both its detractors and supporters call it, also known as the Affordable Care Act (ACA), has been mired in controversy. To cite but one indicator, a nationwide survey conducted by the Kaiser Health Tracking Poll only two weeks before open enrollment in the ACA health insurance exchanges was scheduled to end on March 31, 2014, found that only 38 percent of respondents expressed a favorable view about the healthcare law,[1] despite a massive public-relations push by the White House and its congressional allies. Not only has the American public not embraced the ACA, but calls to "repeal and replace" still echo across the land. What *should* reformers offer in place of the president's healthcare overhaul?

Most critics of the ACA have not systematically identified its flaws or offered a practical, comprehensive market-based alternative to it. In this report, I attempt to remedy that omission by identifying the key problems of the ACA[2] and the solutions that will empower patients, create real competition among health insurers and healthcare providers, and minimize the distorting role of government in the medical marketplace.

Health reform should not be a one-sided affair, an edict imposed from on high onto a hapless polity by legislators who must "pass the legislation in order to know what's in it" (to borrow House Speaker Nancy Pelosi's revealing quip about the ACA). Nor should it be the result of deals struck behind closed doors by career politicians, lobbyists, and special-interest groups. Instead, it should meet the real needs of patients and their doctors and of employees and their employers.

The full case for my proposals can be found in my book *Priceless: Curing the Healthcare Crisis* (Oakland: The Independent Institute, 2012). In fact, this publication is an outgrowth of that book. Given the wider purposes and scope of *Priceless*, I decided that it is a bit too unwieldy to serve the more narrow purpose of explaining what most needs to be done.

A Better Choice spells out the reasoning that undergirds the key pillars on which I believe health reform should rest. Although much of this material draws directly from *Priceless*, I have included additional discussion that sheds light on more recent problems with the ACA. Some of this draws on pieces of mine published at the websites of *Forbes*, *Psychology Today*, and the Independent Institute, and I am delighted that this material is available in a single coherent volume.

PART I

Problems and Principles

2

Six Major Problems of the Affordable Care Act (ACA)

THERE ARE SIX major flaws in the Affordable Care Act (ACA). These cannot be solved by executive order and are not going away unless changed by new legislation. Although this study is primarily a prescription, not a prognosis, a brief review of the ACA's failures is useful for underscoring the need for reforms based on sound principles.

Problem 1: The ACA Imposes an Impossible Mandate

For the past forty years, healthcare spending in the United States has grown at about twice the rate of growth of national income on a real, per capita basis.[3] Although growth in spending slowed modestly after the introduction of Health Savings Accounts (HSAs) and the onset of the Great Recession, there is no reason to think we won't revert back to this trend.[4] The long-term growth in spending is not unique to the United States, nor is the slowdown of recent years. Our healthcare spending growth rate is in the middle of the pack among developed countries.[5] Clearly, the trend cannot go on forever. With each passing year, healthcare crowds out more and more other goods and services that we want to consume. If it were possible to stay on the path we are on, eventually we would have nothing to eat, nothing to wear, and no place to live—but all of us would have a lot of really great healthcare.

President Obama did not create this problem. But the Affordable Care Act will keep us on this path by refusing to allow us to choose better, more efficient insurance alternatives. For example, under the law healthy women with no symptoms are entitled to free mammograms—with no deductible or copayment—even though giving mammograms to healthy women is an increasing controversial activity.[6] However, a woman with actual symptoms that indicate a mammogram is needed may have to pay the full cost ($300 or more) out of pocket.[7] Given the freedom to reverse those provisions, insurers could lower the cost of health insurance and raise the expected quality of care at the same time.

One of the promises of health reform was a more efficient, less costly healthcare system. In pursuit of that goal, the Obama administration is spending millions of dollars on pilot programs and demonstration projects "to find out what works" so those projects can be copied. But the federal government has direct control over only what happens in Medicare. Even there, three Congressional Budget Office reports have concluded that the pilot programs aren't working.[8]

Problem 2: The ACA Makes Promises That Aren't Paid For

While forcing the private sector to buy something that year by year will grow faster than our income, the ACA limits the government's exposure in three ways.

First, under the ACA, Medicare is set to grow only a tiny bit faster than the growth of national income—forever.[9] This provision is reminiscent of an aspect of Congressman Paul Ryan's Medicare reform plan. When Ryan proposed that the "premium support" that seniors get to buy private insurance would grow at a slower rate than the conventional forecast of healthcare costs—thereby shifting more and more of the cost to seniors[10]—Democratic critics howled. Yet this is exactly what the ACA does to all of Medicare. The difference is that the Ryan plan was an undeveloped concept, whereas the ACA is the law of the land.

How does the ACA keep Medicare on this spending path? Absent any successful supply-side changes, Plan B for the ACA is price controls. This implies draconian cuts in Medicare fees for doctors and hospitals[11]—a fact that has been neglected by the mainstream healthcare media.

These cuts by themselves would not reduce total healthcare spending, however, because every dollar of reduced spending on seniors will be used to increase spending on health insurance for young people. Moreover, if seniors react by turning to concierge doctors (described later) and other direct-pay medical services, total spending surely will increase. To make everything even more problematic, many Washington insiders think the spending cuts will never take place. Similar cuts in doctor fees were legislated in 1997, but Congress has postponed the reduction fourteen times.[12] (The "doctor fixes.")

At least as the law is now written, however, spending on the elderly and the disabled will be growing at one rate while the rest of the healthcare system will be growing at twice that rate.

Second, Medicaid hospital expenses are set to grow no faster than Medicare. The Medicare Office of the Actuary included two graphs in the 2012 Medicare Trustees report showing what all this will mean.[13] Figure 2.1 projects approved fees for inpatient hospital services. It shows Medicare and Medicaid fees falling year after year compared to spending by private health insurance. Figure 2.2 shows Medicare-approved fees for doctors dropping below Medicaid fees in the near future, and falling progressively behind Medicaid and private-sector payments indefinitely into the future.[14]

Third, buried deep in the 2,700-page legislation is the little-reported fact that after 2018, subsidies for private health insurance are also scheduled to grow at the same rate as Medicare.

Think about all of this for a moment. The new law will force all of us to purchase health insurance whose cost is likely to grow faster than

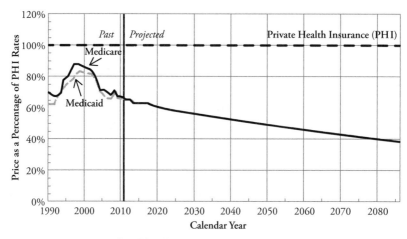

Source: Department of Health and Human Services, Projected Medicare Expenditures under Illustrative Scenarios with Alternative Payment Updates to Medicare Providers

Figure 2.1. Illustrative Comparison of Relative Medicare, Medicaid, and Private Health Insurance Prices for Inpatient Hospital Services under Current Law

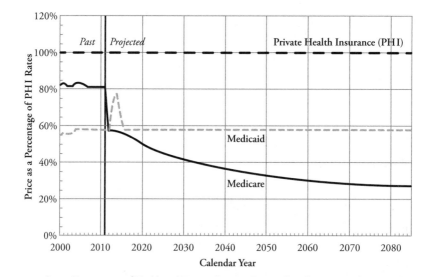

Source: Department of Health and Human Services, Projected Medicare Expenditures under Illustrative Scenarios with Alternative Payment Updates to Medicare Providers

Figure 2.2. Illustrative Comparison of Relative Medicare, Medicaid, and Private Health Insurance Prices for Physician Services under Current Law

our incomes. But government's share of the burden is capped—insuring that more and more of the cost is shifted over time to ordinary citizens.

Problem 3: The ACA Promises What It Cannot Deliver

The healthcare law aims to insure an additional 26 million people. If economic studies are taken as a guide, the newly insured will double their consumption of healthcare.[15] In addition, millions of employees and their employers will be forced to upgrade their health insurance—making it more generous (and more expensive) than before. Again, more insurance coverage inevitably leads to more spending. Then there is a lengthy list of preventive services that must be covered, with no copayment or deductible.[16] Even seniors on Medicare are affected. Although no serious scholar has asserted that it has any medical benefit, seniors are eligible for a free "wellness checkup" every year—all of which will take doctors' time and use valuable resources.[17]

In a 2003 study, researchers at Duke University Medical Center estimated that it would take 1,773 hours a year—or 7.4 hours every working day —for the average doctor to counsel and facilitate patients for every procedure recommended by the U.S. Preventive Services Task Force.[18] And remember, every so often, a screening test turns up something that requires more testing and more doctor time.

The current supply of medical personnel cannot come anywhere close to providing what has been promised, at least for the next 10 to 15 years.[19] In addition, screening tests and similar services add to healthcare costs, rather than reduce them.[20]

What we are describing is a huge increase in the demand for care. But the ACA does nothing to increase supply. This mismatch is virtually guaranteed to put upward pressure on prices. To the extent that prices are prevented from rising, the law will create more rationing by waiting. In other words, your access to care will be controlled by waiting times—

similar to what's happening at the Veterans Administration. And almost anything patients and doctors do to circumvent the cost of waiting will also add to the money cost of care.

For example, a growing number of primary care doctors are turning to concierge practice.[21] For a fee of about $2,000 a year, patients get same-day or next-day appointments, more time with the physician, and someone who will act as their agent in dealing with other parts of a complex healthcare system. Yet physicians who become concierge doctors typically reduce the size of their practice from about 2,500 patients to about 500. So as concierge practices grow, the rationing problem becomes worse for everyone else.

The most vulnerable patients will be those who are in plans that pay below-market fees. These include the elderly and the disabled on Medicare, poor families on Medicaid, and newly insured enrollees in subsidized private plans sold in the health insurance exchanges.[22]

What effects will all of this have on people's health? In the White House, within the Democratic chambers in Congress, and among the (overwhelmingly liberal) health policy community, there was considerable anguish in May 2013. The reason: a study published in the prestigious *New England Journal of Medicine.* Thanks to a state budget crunch in Oregon, scholars were able to perform a double-blind study (the gold standard for researchers), and the findings came out very badly for the supporters of the ACA. Researchers found that (as far as physical health is concerned), there was no difference in outcomes between those enrolled in Medicaid and those who were uninsured.[23] Further, most of the patients went to the emergency room for treatment, rather than to a doctor's office—just as they had before Medicaid enrollment.

(Actually, the results weren't a complete disappointment. Oregon Medicaid enrollees reported less depression, somewhat greater levels of happiness, and among those who had out-of-pocket expenses, savings of about $215 each year. But remember, we could have given the enrollees this amount and spent far less than was actually spent on this program.)

It's hard to exaggerate what a blow this was to the people who gave us the ACA. Everything about the ACA—from the money we are spending to the damage being done to the labor market to the hassles the whole nation is going through—depends on one central idea: that enrolling people in health insurance plans will give them access to better health. (Tens of thousands of lives will be saved every year, the president told us.)

But the gap between rhetoric and reality gets worse. The ACA is expected to insure an additional 26 million people.[24] About half of these will enroll in Medicaid. The other half are supposed to get their insurance in health insurance exchanges, where most will qualify for generous premium subsidies paid for by federal taxpayers. If the Massachusetts health reform is precedent, however, these people will be in health plans that pay doctors about 10 percent more than what Medicaid pays.[25] Think of these plans as Medicaid Plus.

Yet, if Medicaid doesn't make people any healthier than they were when they were uninsured, that implies that the entire ACA program could be one huge waste of money.

Healthcare analysts Aaron Carroll and Austin Frakt argue on their blog, *The Incidental Economist,* that the Oregon study was "underpowered"—failing to show significant effects because there were too few people in each disease category.[26] However, as the *Wall Street Journal* editorial page pointed out, if Oregon's Medicaid program were a drug, it would fail to get FDA approval.[27]

The Oregon study is not the first one to find that enrollees in Medicaid do no better than the uninsured. Other studies have found that Medicaid enrollees find it more difficult to get a doctor's appointment[28] and have worse health outcomes[29] than the uninsured. A 2014 study of the effects of health reform in Massachusetts did find a significant decrease in mortality as a result of health reform in that state.[30]

However, the gains in life expectancy were small relative to the cost.

To a lot of Americans comparing healthcare outcomes with their money cost is an abhorrent idea. But in his book *Critical: What We Can*

Do about the Health-Care Crisis,[31] Tom Daschle, President Obama's first choice to head the Department of Health and Human Resources, said that such healthcare rationing is essential if we are to control costs. Daschle pointed to Britain as a country that routinely does what he had in mind. Other officials associated with the implementation of the ACA are on record expressing similar ideas.

But if it's good to subject all medical procedures to a cost effectiveness standard, isn't it equally good to apply that standard to the entire health reform program? When we do it turns out that the ACA fails the test.

Duke University health economist Chris Conover used estimates of the health gains in Massachusetts as the basis for a calculation and he bent over backwards to make assumptions most favorable to the ACA. "Even under the most wildly optimistic assumptions possible, Obamacare costs a jaw-dropping $224,000 per (quality adjusted) year of additional life," he writes. "In the worst case, the costs would be as high as $1.3 million."[32] This is way beyond the range that Daschle and others consider reasonable. Each of these studies has been subjected to much nitpicking on various grounds, however, and a fair-minded person would probably have to say that how much difference Medicaid makes is an open question.

The authors of the Oregon Medicaid study didn't speculate on the reasons for their findings, but I will. The uninsured in the United States have access to a patchwork system of "free" care when they are unable to pay for it out of their own pockets. In Dallas, Texas, where I live, for example, the entire county is part of a health district that makes indigent healthcare available to needy families. It covers people up to 250 percent of the poverty level, with a sliding scale of copayments, based on family income. Parkland Memorial Hospital and its satellite clinics are the primary providers.

You could argue that uninsured, low-income families in Dallas are actually "insured" in this way, although they face the problems of rationing by waiting and other nonprice barriers to care. Officially, they are counted as "uninsured." However, when these very same individuals enroll in Medicaid, they enter a different system of patchwork care and are classified as "insured." But one-third of the doctors aren't taking any new Medicaid patients.[33] So those who enroll face the same problems of rationing by waiting and other nonprice barriers to care that the uninsured face. Often, the uninsured and Medicaid enrollees get the same care from the same doctors at the same facilities—even though one group is labeled "insured" and the other "uninsured."

Consider the case of Parkland Hospital. Both uninsured and Medicaid patients enter the same emergency room door and see the same doctors. The hospital rooms are the same, the beds are the same, and the care is the same. Consequently, patients have no reason to fill out the lengthy forms and answer the intrusive questions that Medicaid enrollment so often requires. Furthermore, the doctors and nurses who treat these patients are paid the same, regardless of patient' enrollment in an insurance plan. Therefore, they tend to be indifferent about who is insured by whom, and even indifferent about whether they're insured at all. In fact, the only people concerned about who is enrolled in what plan are hospital administrators, who have to pay the bills.

At Children's Medical Center, next door to Parkland, a similar exercise takes place. Medicaid, CHIP, and uninsured children all enter the same emergency room door; they all see the same doctors and receive the same care.

Interestingly, at both institutions, paid staffers make heroic efforts to enroll people in public programs—even as patients wait in the emergency room for medical care. Yet they apparently fail to enroll eligible patients more than half the time. After patients are admitted, staffers valiantly go from room to room to continue this bureaucratic exercise. But even among those in hospital beds, the failure-to-enroll rate is significant—apparently because it has no impact on the care they receive or the financial burden they incur.[34]

Prior to the ACA, more than one-third of all people who were eligible for Medicaid were not enrolled, indicating that millions of potential beneficiaries did not view the program as very valuable.[35] In Oregon, the situation is even more dramatic. Avik Roy wrote the following in 2013:

> Of the 35,169 Oregonians who "won" the lottery to gain enrollment in Medicaid, only about 30 percent actually enrolled. Indeed, only 60 percent of those who were selected bothered to fill out the forms necessary to sign up for the benefits—which tells you a bit about how uninsured Oregonians perceive the Medicaid program.[36]

Now consider Massachusetts. Romneycare cut the official "uninsurance" rate in half. But it created no new doctors or nurses or clinics. Hospital emergency room traffic is higher than ever. The traffic to the community health centers has changed very little.

But since they have expanded health insurance in Massachusetts, the demand for care has grown, even as the supply has remained unchanged. As a result, the time price of care has increased. According to a 2009 survey, the wait to see a new doctor in Boston is two months—the longest waiting time in the entire country.[37] People are getting the same care they got before Romneycare was implemented, but they are paying a higher "time price" for it. I expect to see the Massachusetts results replicated nationwide.

In the developed world, the health policy community is excessively focused on health *insurance,* even to the point of ignoring *healthcare.* In fact, studies of waiting times and the inability to get care are often derided as right-wing attempts to undermine the concept of social insurance. The less-developed world has the opposite vision. Almost all the countries south of our border offer free care to the general population, but they don't hand everyone an insurance card.[38]

I believe that this difference in vision is partly explained by the difference in income and wealth. Middle- and upper-middle-income families need insurance to protect their assets. Poor families don't have assets. They don't need insurance. They do need healthcare, however.

The ACA was designed by middle- and upper-middle-income people. They chose for poor people the same thing they would want for themselves. They didn't think about access to care because they have never had a personal problem with it.

Problem 4: The ACA Subsidies and Mandates Will Destabilize Entire Sectors of the Economy

The ACA confers large benefits on some people and imposes large costs on others, even at the same income level. In many states, a family at 138 percent of the poverty level will qualify for expanded Medicaid. Since Medicaid is expected to spend $8,000 on an average family of four over the course of a year, a family's enrollment is like getting an $8,000 gift from the government. If the family earns $1 more, however, they will no longer be eligible for Medicaid and must buy insurance in a health insurance exchange. Let's say they obtain a $12,000 family plan for no more than about a $900 premium. This is like getting an $11,100 gift.

Now consider people at work. A typical hotel worker tends to earn about $15 to $20 an hour—the housekeeping staff, the waiters and waitresses, the busboys, the porters, the custodians, the groundskeepers, and so on. Yet the cost of family coverage from a typical employer is equal to about one-half of these workers' annual earnings. The goal of the ACA is to force them to obtain this insurance with no extra help from government. And this is true even if the housekeepers are already enrolled in Medicaid. If the employer doesn't provide it, the firm will be fined $2,000 per worker per year.

To recap: Families at roughly the same income level can get an $8,000 gift, an $11,100 gift, or a $2,000 fine. Clearly, this is arbitrary and unfair. And it has the potential to affect the entire structure of various industries in a very negative way.

Why do I say that a fine paid by the employer is really paid by the employee? Regardless of how much of a health insurance premium or a fine for not providing health insurance is paid by an employer, the economic effects are the same, regardless of who writes the checks. The economic literature on this type of mandate is clear. Although government can offer people something for nothing, the labor market does not. Employee benefits are not gifts from employers. They are substitutes for money wages and other benefits. The cost of the employer-provided insurance or the fine will ultimately be borne by the employees themselves. For example, health economist Mark Pauly and his colleagues at the Wharton School at the University of Pennsylvania have shown mandated health insurance in Massachusetts was offset dollar for dollar by lower cash wages.[39]

We can be fairly certain that low-wage workers and their employers will be searching for ways to avoid the mandate. How can we be so confident? Because if the employees were willing to spend half of their income on health insurance, they would have done so already. That they have not indicates they would rather spend the money on something else.

The Congressional Budget Office estimates that the cost of the minimum benefit package everyone will be required to have will be $4,750 for individuals and $12,250 for families. That translates into a minimum health benefit of $2.28 an hour for full-time single workers and about $3 an hour for someone working 30 hours a week. For family coverage the cost is $5.89 an hour for a 40-hour-a-week employee and $7.85 an hour for a 30-hour-a-week employee.

These are not small changes, and in some instances they can double the cost of labor. The ACA mandate begins applying to larger employers, with more than 100 employees, in 2015 and to smaller employers, with 50 to 99 employees,33 in 2016. For those who are already providing generous coverage to above-average income employees, this will not be much of a burden. But for those who provide limited insurance or no health insurance to below-average income employees, the burden may be extremely onerous.

How Employers Are Responding to the Mandate

Employers face the following options:

Stay Small

As long as employers restrict their workforces to no more than forty-nine employees the mandate doesn't apply. But here is a warning: the IRS has signaled that if an individual owns, say, three separate businesses, it will treat them as one business—not three. In this way, the ACA will discourage not only small businesses from growing, but also entrepreneurs from acquiring or starting other businesses.

For employers who try to use part-time labor to stay under the 50 employee mark, the IRS has another surprise: it will count "full-time equivalents." For example, it will count two 15-hour-a-week employees as equivalent to one full-time employee in determining the relevant number of employees.

Use Part-Time Labor

Even if the mandate applies, the employer does not have to offer insurance to employees who work fewer than 30 hours a week. That's one reason why part-time jobs are soaring while full-time employment is stagnating. But employers shouldn't wait until the year the mandate becomes effective to make decisions about their workforce. The IRS can look back to the prior 12 months to determine whether or not an employee has full-time status.

One firm I talked with, managing about one hundred fast-food restaurants, had an average workweek of 38 hours in 2012. In January 2013 they shifted to an average of 25 hours. At that time, everyone expected the mandate to take effect in January 2014.

Making sure that employees stay under the 30-hour bar will require vigilance. And mistakes can be costly. If a 29-hour-a-week employee works one more hour for 50 weeks that will trigger a $2,000 fine. Dividing the fine by the additional hours of work, translates into a $40-an-hour penalty.

For their part, employees may be able to avoid a cut in take-home pay by working part-time for two different employers—both of which avoid the mandate by switching to part-time labor. This is apparently happening in the fast food industry.

Use Non-Employee Labor

Independent contractors by definition are not employees. As long as they don't work regular hours, workers can retain their status as contractors even if they work at the employer's establishment. The temp business began to boom in anticipation of the mandate taking effect.[40] Outsourcing is another strategy. As one business owner has explained, "There is almost nothing that cannot be outsourced."

Charge Employees the Maximum Allowable Premium

Under the new law, health insurance is deemed "affordable" if the employee's share of the premium does not exceed 9.5 percent of the employee's wages. If the offer is rejected, the employer is off the hook—no health insurance costs and no government fine. Take an employee earning $30,000 a year. Insurance is considered affordable so long as the employee pays no more than $2,850, or 9.5 percent of income. If the employer's cost of providing individual coverage is $4,500, the employer has to pay only $1,650. The employee will pay more than half the cost. Under the ACA, the employer doesn't have to contribute anything to cover the employee's dependents. Let's say the employer offers family coverage that costs $15,000. The employer can ask the employee to pay $12,150, with the employer (again) paying only $1,650. If the employee accepts the offer, the employer is out only $1,650. (Remember: the employer fine for not offering any insurance is $2,000.)

To add insult to injury, the employee's contribution in all likelihood will be made with after-tax dollars, whereas the employer's share, if the offer is accepted, will be paid with before-tax dollars. And here is the cruel upshot of all this: Once the employer has offered "affordable" health insurance (even though it really isn't affordable), the employee and his family are no longer entitled to a subsidy in the exchange. If they buy coverage—even a bronze plan—they will have to pay the full price.

Unfortunately, what is in the self-interest of the employer can be very harmful to the employee and his/her family.

Offer a Minimum Essential Coverage (MEC) Plan

Self-insured employers (who cover more than half of all employees with health insurance) have another option. As long as they offer insurance with minimum essential coverage (mainly preventive care with no cost sharing and no lifetime caps), a self-insured employer can escape the $2,000 fine. The remaining benefits can be quite skimpy, however. But note: since this plan does not meet other requirements of the ACA mandate for employers, the employer will be liable for a $3,000 fine if an employee develops a serious illness and goes to the exchange to get a richer, subsidized plan.

Ralph Weber is an employee benefits specialist in Houston and the founder and CEO of Medibid. According to Weber, the trick here is to make the plan attractive enough so that otherwise healthy, low-wage workers don't go to the exchange for insurance. This might be a skimpy plan, which covers doctor visits and generic drugs but excludes inpatient surgery and ER visits. If an employee develops a serious illness, she is likely to go to the exchange to get a richer, subsidized plan. However, the $3,000 fine the employer will then have to pay may be a bargain compared to the cost of treating the illness.

Offer a MEC Plan with an Opportunity to Upgrade to ACA Compatible Insurance

Weber is also helping employers with another option. They can offer an upgrade to a plan that meets the "affordability" test and the "minimum actuarial value" test (see below). To meet the affordability test the employee's premium (again, employee coverage only—not family) must not exceed 9.5 percent of the annual wage. If the employee turns down the offer, the employer is no longer at risk for a $3,000 fine. And if the employee becomes ill and goes to the exchange for coverage, he and his family will no longer qualify for any federal subsidy. Again, what's good for the employer is bad for the employee and vice versa.

Take Advantage of Imperfections in the Minimum Value Calculator

In addition to being affordable, health insurance must meet a "minimum actuarial value" test. For self-insured companies, this means that the benefits can differ from the essential health benefits included in a standard plan, but the employer plan has to cover at least 60 percent of expected costs under a standard plan.

One official way to do that is to get a passing score on the Department of Health and Human Services' "minimum-value" calculator, an online tool. And here is a surprise: an employer can actually meet this test without including hospitalization! In a rear-guard regulatory move, the Obama administration now says it will require hospitalization anyway. But employers are off the hook for such other essential visits as specialist care and ER visits.[41]

Pay the Fine

Employers can drop health insurance coverage altogether (or never provide it in the first place) and pay a fine equal to $2,000 per employee. That's a stiff price to pay, but it's less than the cost of health insurance. If the employer chooses this option, the employees will be eligible for subsidized insurance in the exchange.

Overall Impact on the Labor Market

Case Study: The Fast Food Industry

By the end of 2015, we may discover that workers who earn within a few dollars of the minimum wage have less income and less insurance coverage (as a group) than they did the before the mandate began to take effect. This conclusion is based on my study of 136 fast-food restaurants.

They initially employed close to 3500 workers, about half of whom were full time (30 hours or more a week). The potential cost to the employers of providing mandated health insurance to the full time staff was about $7 million a year. But by the time the employers took advantage of all their legal options they were able to reduce their cost to less than 1 percent of that amount.

Here's how they did it.

The first step was to make all hourly workers part time. That may seem like an easy thing to do, but it's not. In the fast food business it's not uncommon for employees not to show up for work. That means other employees are asked to work additional hours to prevent the restaurant from shutting down. By year end, 58 employees (about 3 percent) had crossed the line and were eligible for mandated health insurance the following year.

For these employees, the companies offered Obamacare-compliant health insurance (Bronze plans), but they asked the employees to pay the maximum premium the law allows: 9.5 percent of their annual wage. For a $9-an-hour employee working 30 hours a week, the maximum monthly premium is $111. Since the total premium is $367, the employer is required to pay the difference.

This type of plan has very large deductibles and copayments, however—up to $6,600 of exposure ($13,200 for a family). High deductible health insurance (with no Health Savings Account) is not attractive to young, healthy, low-income workers, however. They are far more likely to prefer "mini med" plans that pay for generic drugs and doctor visits, but not catastrophic care.

In fact, prior to the Obamacare mandate, these companies offered their employees a standard Blue Cross plan and a mini med plan for a much lower premium. No one signed up for the Blue Cross plan. About 200 signed up for mini med insurance.

As an alternative to the Bronze plan, the employers are now offering a Minimum Essential Coverage (MEC) plan—basically, a type of mini med insurance that covers preventive care and very little else (no hospitalization, no specialist care, etc.). The companies in my survey offered to pay the full premium for the mini med plans, in order to make that alternative more attractive. If employees choose the Bronze plan it costs the employers about six times as much.

As noted, employees who sign up for MEC coverage escape the threatened Obamacare fine for being "uninsured." And the employers are also off the hook for any fine in this case because they offered all full-time employees a Bronze plan, even if the employees turned it down.

The result: out of 58 remaining full-time employees, only one enrolled in a Bronze plan; the rest will likely be in MEC plans.

What about workers' families? As noted, employers have no obligation to pay the premiums for dependent coverage. For a family of three, the employee can face a premium of $805 a month—almost 70 percent of his monthly wage! And since Obamacare considers this offer "affordable," if it is turned down neither the employee nor his family is eligible for subsidized insurance in the health insurance exchange.

What about the mini med plans? Although these plans are offered for free to the employees, dependent coverage is not free. In fact, the employee has to pay about 25 percent of his income to cover a spouse and kid. If they don't, they will face a fine next April 15.

Let's return to all the employees whose hours were reduced to part time. They can get subsidized insurance in the exchange. But remember: they will be asked to pay up to a tenth of their take-home pay for what is very unattractive insurance. Some of them previously had mini med plans, but this kind of insurance is no longer available to them.

So let's recap. Almost half the work force of these restaurants was involuntarily reduced to part time and has less income as a result. All but a handful of employees has lost the opportunity to have the insurance they most prefer: mini med plans that pay for medical care they are most likely to need. And those who do get mini med insurance from their employer will have dependents who are not covered, who will not be able to get insurance in the exchange, and who will face a fine for being uninsured.

Out of 3,500 employees, only one that we know of got the kind of insurance that the Obamacare creators wanted everyone to have.

Many employers won't want to get out of the health insurance business altogether. One reason is that their incentives reverse for high-income employees. Someone making, say, $90,000 will never qualify for Medicaid. If he goes into the exchange, he will get no subsidy. But if he gets insurance at work, the employer's premium payments avoid a 25-percent income tax, a 15-percent payroll tax, and state and local income taxes as well.

These differential subsidies will have a big impact on our economy. As businesses discover that almost everyone who earns less than the average wage gets a better deal from the federal government in the exchange or from Medicaid, whereas most people who earn more than the average wage get a better deal if insurance is provided at work, trends already evident will accelerate. Higher-income workers will tend to congregate in firms that provide insurance; lower-income workers will tend to work for firms that do not. But efficient production requires that firm size and labor-force composition be determined by economic factors, not health-insurance subsidies.

The ACA retained the subsidies in the current tax system, under which government effectively pays almost half the cost of insurance for higher-income employees. How can employers provide insurance to those who earn above the average while avoiding coverage for workers earning below-average wages? That is another challenge employers face.

Ask almost any employer, and there won't be much doubt: the ACA raises the cost of labor, discourages hiring, and has a negative effect on the economy. Three Federal Reserve Banks—in Philadelphia, New York, and Atlanta—have released business surveys that confirm this. The new health law is discouraging a significant number of firms from hiring and is also pushing workers into part-time, rather than full time jobs.

The Federal Reserve Bank of Philadelphia survey of business in its region finds that because of the ACA:

- 18.2 percent of employers say they cut workers versus 3.0 percent who hired more.
- 18.2 percent say the proportion of part-time workers is higher versus 1.5 percent who say it is lower.
- 13.7 percent reported more outsourcing to other firms versus 3 percent with less outsourcing.[42]

The New York Fed conducted two surveys in its region. Because of the ACA:

- 21 percent of manufacturers say they are reducing employment, while 3 percent are increasing their workforce.
- In the business leaders survey on the same issue the responses were 16.9 percent versus 1.6 percent.
- Among manufacturers, 19.3 percent say they are increasing the proportion of part-time work, while 3.5 percent say they are reducing it.
- In the business leaders survey on the same question the numbers are 20.2 percent versus 4.8 percent.[43]

An Atlanta Fed poll found that 34 percent of businesses planned to hire more part-time workers than in the past, mostly because of a rise in the relative costs of their full-time colleagues.[44]

As for the impact of the ACA on healthcare costs, the New York survey is especially instructive:

- More than one-third of manufacturers say the ACA is increasing costs "a lot" this year and more than half say the health law will increase costs a lot next year.
- Among New York business leaders, more than one in four say the ACA is increasing costs a lot this year and more than one-third predict substantial cost increases next year.

- Employers are responding by shifting more of the direct costs to the employees. They are using deductibles and copayments and asking employees to pay a larger share of the premium.[45]

Economists who favor the ACA have pushed back, however. In 2011, David Cutler of Harvard University testified before the House of Representatives Committee on Energy and Commerce, arguing that the ACA would reduce average healthcare costs by about 5 percent by 2015.[46] This, he said, would decrease the cost of labor for employers and increase nationwide employment. Cutler also organized and signed an economists' letter to Congress, asserting that "repealing the ACA would produce job reductions of 250,000 to 400,000 annually."[47]

But how much of this pushback is just politics, as opposed to real economics? Although Cutler is an able healthcare economist, he's not an expert in labor economics. Someone who is at the top of that field is University of Chicago economist Casey Mulligan, who took Cutler to task for ignoring all of the ways in which the ACA discourages hiring, full-time employment, and businesses that hope to grow. At the *New York Times* Economix blog on August 7, 2013, Mulligan wrote the following:

> Neither Professor Cutler's testimony nor the economists' letter mentioned that the ACA also creates explicit taxes on employers, subsidies for layoffs and various implicit taxes on employees with many of the same economic characteristics as taxes on employers.[48]

According to Mulligan:

> the tax effects that Professor Cutler left out are about 10 times greater than, and in the opposite direction of, those he conveyed to Congress. . . . If his estimate of the cost-savings channel is accurate, and I am right that the overall labor market effect of the act is about 10 times larger (in the other direction) than the cost-savings channel, we might then expect the act to contract the 2015 labor market by about 3 percent rather than expand it.[49]

That represents a loss of 4 million jobs.

Cutler offered a rejoinder to Mulligan in which he argued that the ACA will have the following positive effects on the job market:

- Easy access to health insurance eliminates "job lock" and frees workers to move along to a more productive job or to start a business.
- Greater access to health insurance encourages people on disability insurance to work more often.
- Also, there are the costs of workers missing work (absenteeism) or being less productive at work because they are ill.[50]

Even so, these positive benefits are likely to be overwhelmed by the negative aspects of the law—burdens that were never necessary in the first place, if the only goal was to help the uninsured get health insurance.

Problem 5: The ACA Creates Perverse Incentives That Threaten the Quality of Care

Under the ACA, health insurers are no longer permitted to consider an individual's health status in determining their premiums, and they are required to accept anyone who applies. This means that they must overcharge the healthy and undercharge the sick. It also means that they have strong incentives to attract the healthy (on whom they make a profit) and avoid the sick (on whom they incur losses).

Attracting the Healthy, Avoiding the Sick

Before the ACA went fully into effect, insurers in most states were allowed to charge individuals premiums that reflected their expected healthcare costs. This practice is no different than it is in life insurance, casualty insurance, or almost any other kind of insurance—although since these other forms of insurance are not usually obtained through employers, people don't lose coverage when they switch jobs. In a free market, you expect to pay premiums that are actuarially fair. The ACA ended this practice. Instead, insurers are required to practice a form of community rating, under which the healthy and the sick are charged the same rate. (The ACA permits insurers to consider only four factors in setting their rates: individual versus family enrollment, geographic area, age, and tobacco use.)

You don't have to be in the health insurance business to understand what kind of incentives the ACA rate restrictions create for the insurers. It is in the self-interest of every insurer to attract the healthy and avoid the sick. How might they do that? One way is to design plans that on the surface are more appealing to the healthy than to the sick.

Traditional insurance theory holds that patients should pay out of pocket for expenses that are small and over which they have a great deal of discretion. Insurance, on the other hand, should pay for expenses that are large and over which patients don't have much discretion. The insurance offered in the ACA exchanges turns that theory on its head, however.

Under a typical California plan, for example, patients will make only nominal copayments when they see a doctor or get a blood test or X-ray exam—measures that are often discretionary and the source of a great deal of unnecessary care.[51] But if they go into a hospital, where patients have almost no control over what is done and no prior knowledge of what anything costs, they will be charged from 10 percent to 20 percent of the total bill. For an individual earning only a few thousand dollars above the poverty level, a hospital visit will cost $2,500. For a lower-middle-income patient, the charge will be $6,350. A moderate-income family can end up paying hospital expenses of $12,500—every year. Clearly, this plan will be attractive to people who don't plan to enter a hospital and unattractive to people for whom a hospital stay is likely.

Race to the Bottom on Access to Care

Think of an insurance plan as having three main components: (1) a premium, (2) a list of covered benefits, and (3) a network of doctors, hospitals, and other providers. Under the ACA, there is very strict regulation of benefits that insurers must offer—right down to free contraceptives, questionable mammograms, and non-cost-effective preventive procedures. At the same time, health plans have been given enormous freedom to set their own (community-rated) premiums and choose their own networks. They are using that freedom in yet another way to attract the healthy and avoid the sick.

In the ACA exchanges, the insurers apparently believe that only sick people (who plan to spend a lot of healthcare dollars) pay close attention to networks. Healthy people tend to buy on price. Thus, by keeping fees so low that only a minority of physicians will agree to treat the patients, some insurers are able to quote very low premiums. They are banking on attracting the healthy, and they may even have the good luck to scare away the sick.

Consider the incentives on the buyer side. In the ACA exchanges, if I am healthy, why wouldn't I buy on price? If I later develop cancer, I'll move to a plan that has the best cancer care. If I develop heart disease, I'll enter a plan with the best heart doctors. And these new plans will be prohibited from charging me more than the premium paid by a healthy enrollee. (For a more comprehensive look, see Chapter 22 from my 2004 book with Gerald Musgrave and Devon Herrick, *Lives at Risk: Single-Payer National Health Insurance Around the World.*[52])

As a result, we are getting a race to the bottom on access[53]—with private plans in the exchanges looking increasingly like Medicaid, just as they do in Massachusetts.[54] The Obama administration doesn't seem to be bothered by this development. In fact, it has touted the fact that the premiums have been lower than expected,[55] even though the reason is that the networks are narrower and skimpier than expected.

Think how different this is from what we were promised. During the 2008 election, every serious candidate for the Democratic presidential nomination parroted the "universal coverage" mantra over and over again—and on the left "universal coverage" means universal access to care. No candidate even hinted that access to *providers* might not be any better than under Medicaid.

Problem 6: A Weakly Enforced Mandate Will Undermine the Health Insurance Marketplace

The penalty for a nonexempt individual who has not obtained health insurance is relatively small: $95 or 1 percent of income in 2014. In future years the penalty increases, but for most people it will never come close to the cost of the health insurance they are required to buy. Further, the enforcement mechanism is weak. All the IRS can do is withhold your income tax refund. It can't garnish your wages or attach an asset or even require you to pay a higher tax. And if you manage your affairs smartly, you will never be owed a refund.

As a result, the great fear of the Obama administration (and indeed the entire health insurance industry) was that millions of healthy people would avoid enrolling in the insurance exchanges during the first open-enrollment period. That possibility was made more likely by a long, complicated enrollment form and an arduous enrollment procedure. Unless you are really sick and need health insurance immediately, the temptation will be to wait to enroll until you have a healthcare problem. To make matters worse, the healthy, remember, are being overcharged from the beginning.

In Massachusetts, people who game the system are called "jumpers" and "dumpers." They wait until they are sick to enroll and "jump in." Then, after they get the care they need and get their medical bills paid, they drop their coverage. Of course, if the only people who have health insurance are people who are sick, the cost of insurance will go right through the roof.

To combat this possibility, the Obama administration launched a desperate offensive prior to the exchanges' initial open-enrollment period, enlisting professional athletes, Hollywood actors, rock stars, librarians, and anybody else who could help persuade the healthy, especially the young and healthy, to join up.

Without a sufficient percentage of healthy enrollees, a state exchange could become vulnerable to a death spiral, which occurs when pricing in an insurance market spins out of control. If an insurance pool turns out to be more expensive than originally thought, the insurer must raise its premiums. As the premium rises, some healthy people drop their coverage. With a sicker group of enrollees, the average cost per enrollee will be higher, and premiums must be increased again. That leads more healthy people to drop out—leading to more premium increases. This cycle continues until the only people left in the pool are very sick and very expensive to insure. They must be charged a premium that roughly equals the cost of their care. But this is a premium they can't afford, of course, and so it is a premium the insurer cannot collect. The ultimate end of a death spiral is the insurance pool equivalent of bankruptcy.

One reason for a death spiral is government price fixing, usually in the form of community rating and guaranteed issue (where everyone is charged the same premium and the insurer must take all comers). Healthy people leave the pool because they are being overcharged. Sick people remain because they are being undercharged. This would not occur if each enrollee were charged a premium that reflects her actuarial risk.

Death spirals can also happen in an unregulated insurance market. They can occur, for example, if insurers offer to renew coverage indefinitely without adjusting individual premiums for changes in health conditions, while the enrollees are free to leave and find cheaper insurance if their health condition is better than average.

The threat of a death spiral in the exchanges is made worse by five developments.

First, state risk pools and the federal (ACA) risk pools have closed and dumped their high-cost enrollees on the health insurance exchanges. On January 1, 2014, for example, the State of Texas formally ended its risk pool, and the 23,000 people who were enrolled have presumably sought coverage in the Texas exchange.[56] It was a good deal for the state, which had been spending more than $12,000 per enrollee operating the pool.[57] Other states have followed suit. So have the ACA risk pools—some run by state governments and some run by the federal government—which were insuring about 107,000 people.[58]

Second, public and private employers are poised to dump their retirees onto the exchanges. City governments across the country have promised post-retirement healthcare benefits to retirees who are not yet eligible for Medicare. This is the age group that is the most expensive to cover. Under the ACA, the exchanges have federal subsidies, and the law limits the premiums to no more than three times the premium charged to enrollees in their twenties (although the actual cost of coverage is more on the order of six to one). Detroit, for example, is sending 8,000 city retirees to the Michigan exchange.[59]

The private sector is following suit. According to a Towers Watson survey, more than half of employers that offer healthcare benefits to pre-65-year-old retirees plan to discontinue them.[60]

Third, workers are no longer trapped in jobs they might otherwise have left because their health conditions would have caused them to pay much higher premiums in the individual market or to be denied insurance altogether. Millions of people can now leave their employer plans and enroll in the exchange, paying premiums well below the expected cost of their care.

Fourth, people can game the system from within the exchange. That is, they can buy a cheaper silver or bronze plan while they are healthy and then upgrade to platinum or gold if they develop a serious illness.

Finally, employers that self-insure (covering more than half of all insured workers) have options not available to other employers. Using techniques we described previously, they will find ways to dump their sickest employees on the exchange.

What should the designers of the ACA have done to avoid the problems we are describing here? They should have followed some common-sense principles.

3

Six Principles for Commonsense Reform

IN REFORMING THE ACA, there are six principles that should be adhered to. They are compatible with a free-market approach to healthcare reform. As we shall see, these provisions hold the key that would unlock the door to high-quality, affordable healthcare for all.

Principle 1: Choice

People should be free to choose a health plan that fits individual and family needs, rather than one designed by bureaucrats in Washington. This means no mandate. Men shouldn't have to buy maternity coverage; women shouldn't have to buy coverage for prostate cancer tests; and teetotalers shouldn't have to buy substance abuse insurance. No one should have to buy coverage for preventive procedures that health researchers have known for years are not cost-effective.

Had we accepted the principle of choice in designing health reform, millions of policy holders in the individual market would have been spared the shock and hassle of losing plans they were promised they could keep, and millions more with coverage through their employers would have been spared the fear of losing their plans, as well.

Principle 2: Fairness

Fairness means that if government subsidizes health insurance, then the subsidy should be the same for everyone at the same income level. Moreover, I believe a strong case can be made that the subsidy should be in the form of a fixed sum tax credit and that everyone, regardless of income, should get the same tax credit. For example, we could offer every adult an annual tax credit worth $2,500 and every child a credit worth $1,500. People would get this subsidy so long as they obtained credible private health insurance, no matter where they obtained it—at work, in the marketplace, or in an exchange.

With a uniform tax credit, 90 percent of the problems with the ACA exchanges would vanish. Signing up for insurance would be easy. Insurance companies and brokers would be able to enroll people outside of the exchanges without asking privacy-invading questions about their income and assets.

Principle 3: Universal Coverage

There will always be some people who will turn down the offer of a tax credit. Instead of having the U.S. Treasury keep those unclaimed credits, some portion of the money should be sent to safety-net institutions in the communities where the uninsured live. Uninsured patients will probably be asked to pay their medical bills out of their own pockets. But if they cannot, the safety-net institutions will have a source of cash to pay for "uncompensated care."

Note: The tax credit dollar amounts stated previously are the Congressional Budget Office's estimates of the cost of enrolling new people in Medicaid. So one way of thinking about the credits is to see that they will fund insurance that looks a lot like Medicaid. To obtain more accessible care or better care, people would have to add their own funds to the tax credit amount. An additional way of ensuring universal coverage would be to allow people to use their tax credit to buy into Medicaid, regardless of income.

Principle 4: Portability

In most states today, it is illegal for employers to buy for their employees what they most want and need—insurance that travels with them from job to job and in and out of the labor market. Employers can buy group insurance with pretax dollars. But they can't buy individually owned insurance on behalf of their employees. This prohibition means that people lose their insurance when they leave their employer, and this was the primary reason why developing a preexisting condition in the past could cause families much financial hardship. The prohibition must be repealed.

Employers should be encouraged to provide portable insurance for their employees in the same way that 401(k) plans and employer-paid life insurance are portable. NFL football players and members of the United Mine Workers already have portable insurance, with premiums paid by their employers. It's unconscionable that our laws prevent the vast majority of people from having that same option.

Principle 5: Patient Power

Health Savings Accounts (HSAs) and Health Reimbursement Arrangements (HRAs) are very effective ways to eliminate waste and control costs. That's why 30 million people now have these accounts. Still, we are not taking full advantage of the opportunities here.

Current law imposes rigid restrictions on HSAs. Those restrictions should be lifted so that HSAs are allowed to be completely flexible—wrapping around any third-party insurance plan. Then let the market determine the appropriate division between third-party insurance and individual self-insurance in the form of a designated savings account. The private sector also should be able to create special accounts for the chronically ill. A model for this is Medicaid's highly successful Cash and Counseling program, under which the homebound disabled manage their own healthcare dollars.

Principle 6: Real Insurance

The primary goal of the ACA was to give everyone access to healthcare. Yet the way things are panning out, millions of people are losing insurance with very reasonable access to providers and are being forced into an exchange where the typical health plan avoids the best doctors and the best hospitals. In some areas, these plans are dubbed "Medicaid Plus."

How could things be different? Let people insure against the costs of getting a preexisting condition. Under this approach, no insurer would be allowed to dump its most costly enrollees onto another insurer without paying the full cost of the transfer. So if an expensive-to-treat patient moves from Plan A to Plan B, the former has to compensate the latter for any above-average expected costs. This "change-of-health-status insurance" would eliminate the financial hardship associated with developing a preexisting condition.[61]

What would it cost to create an alternative to the ACA based on these six principles? I believe that if we take all of the current subsidies for employer-provided insurance and add all of the subsidies the ACA is providing, there is more than enough money for the reforms I recommend.

PART II

Taking a Closer Look at the Principles

4

Understanding Choice

THE FEDERAL MANDATE requiring most Americans to obtain health insurance is perhaps the most well known provision of the ACA. The mandate became effective for most people beginning on January 1, 2014. Not only does the government require that you have health insurance, but it also determines the type of coverage you have, where you will get it, and how much you will pay for it.

Among the problems: The mandate encourages waste, limits the ability of insurance to meet our individual needs, reduces the ability of employers to offer higher wages and other benefits, and even puts many jobs at risk.

Encouraging Wasteful Spending

Real health costs per capita have been rising at twice the rate of real per capita income for the past forty years. Nor is this a uniquely American problem.[62] All over the developed world, healthcare spending has been consuming more and more of income with each passing year.

President Obama did not create the underlying problem. But the ACA is likely to make matters worse by disallowing normal consumer reactions to rising premiums. For example, most people would react to unaffordable premiums by choosing a more limited package of benefits, opting for catastrophic coverage only, or relying more on Health Savings Accounts to pay for primary care and diagnostic tests. But these and other responses are limited or barred altogether under the new law.

To people who subscribe to the health policy orthodoxy, the riddle of modern healthcare is: Why have healthcare costs increased so much? To me the riddle is: Why aren't we spending even more?

Every time you and I spend a dollar at a physician's office, only 10 cents is coming out of our own pockets, on the average.[63] The remainder is paid by a third party—an employer, an insurance company, or the government. That means our incentive is to consume healthcare until the last unit purchased is worth to us only 10 cents on the dollar. That's enormously wasteful. It means we are consuming healthcare that is worth 10 cents when, with the same money, we could have consumed something worth one dollar. Why do we do that? Because we are trapped in a third-party payer system with use-it-or-lose-it benefits. Most of the time our health plan doesn't give us the option to buy less healthcare and more of something else.

The ACA has strengthened our incentives to overconsume. Insurers must cover fifteen preventive services (mammograms, Pap smears, colonoscopies, etc.) without any copayment or deductible.[64] Yet if the cost of these services to us is zero at the time we consume them, our incentive will be to consume them until the last bit is almost worthless. Also, because no out-of-pocket payment is required, no one has any incentive to comparison shop and try to minimize the cost of these services. Could some preventive care be provided at lower cost by a nurse at a walk-in clinic rather than at a doctor's office? Undoubtedly. But the ACA prevents you from having a health plan that gives you economic incentives to economize and reduce costs in that way.

Some readers may be skeptical of the idea that people will overuse the healthcare system. Are we talking about a few hypochondriacs? Or, are we talking about ordinary people? The latter. In Florida, for example, the waiting rooms of many specialist doctors are gathering places for senior citizens who take the occasion to socialize and enjoy each other's company.

The reality is that these services are not costless. In fact, the way our system functions, most healthcare is very expensive. So although we consume care as though it were free, we all end up paying a very steep price through higher premiums and higher taxes.

As a practical matter, once we pay insurance premiums, that money is combined with everyone else's premiums in a pool. Once the money is in the pool, it is no longer "ours." When we draw from the pool, we are spending everybody's money. Moreover, the only way to get benefits from the health insurance pool is to spend money on medical care.

If you and I are in the same insurance pool, consider how many ways there are for me to spend your money:

- If my wife and I decide to have another child and we have fertility problems, there's always in-vitro fertilization. Cost: $20,000.
- If we decide not to have a child, there is always a vasectomy or tubal ligation. Cost: $1,000 to $7,000.
- If I decide that my thinning hair needs thickening, there's Propecia at an annual cost of $842.
- If my testosterone level isn't in sync with my idealized vision of my own virility, there is Androgel. Cost: $831 per year.
- If my unhealthy diet leads to diabetes, many of those costs will become "ours" as well. Average annual extra cost: $7,000.

Notice that I haven't even mentioned yet the normal diagnostic screenings (PSA test, colonoscopy, etc.). They cost money as well. Then, let's say that over time, I abuse my body with alcohol, tobacco, drugs, fatty foods, lack of exercise, and so on. I know that others will pay my medical costs—mainly from first dollar—once I get old enough to qualify for Medicare.

Limiting the Ability to Meet Individual Needs

Well before the ACA went into effect, mandated benefits made insurance premiums unaffordable for many consumers. Studies show that as many as one out of four uninsured Americans—most of them healthy—have been priced out of the market for health insurance by cost-increasing, mandated benefits.[65] At the same time, however, these mandates raise premiums for the chronically ill and divert dollars away from their care. There is no reason that a diabetic should have to pay for other peoples' in-vitro fertilization, naturopathy, acupuncture, or marriage counseling, in order to obtain diabetic care.

Crowding Out Wage Increases

Most people will continue to obtain health insurance through an employer. The Congressional Budget Office estimates the average annual cost of a minimum benefit package at $4,500 to $5,000 for individuals and $12,000 to $12,500 for families in 2016.[66] Thus, the minimum cost of labor will be a $7.25 cash minimum wage and a $5.89 health minimum wage (family), for a total of $13.14 an hour or about $27,331 a year.

Imagine that you are an employer. You certainly aren't going to pay an employee more than his or her value to the organization, and competition from other employers will tend to prevent you from paying less. If the government forces you to spend more on health insurance, you will spend less in wages in order to pay for the mandated benefits.

For above-average-wage employees, the consequence of all this is straightforward. Expect wage stagnation over the foreseeable future, as employers use potential wage increases to pay for expanded (and mandated) health benefits instead. At the low end of the wage scale, however, the effects of the ACA will be devastating.

Crowding Out Jobs

Ten-dollar-an-hour workers and their employers cannot afford $6-an-hour health insurance. If they bought it, only $4 would be left for cash wages, and that would violate the (cash) minimum wage law. This is not a small problem. One-third of uninsured workers earn less than $3 above the minimum wage.[67]

Further, although health economists have known for decades that low-wage earners are the workers who most need help in obtaining insurance, no new subsidies are provided to help employees at Walmart or McDonald's or Denny's or any other restaurant chain buy health insurance. These workers and many others are at risk of losing their jobs.

Do We Really Need a Mandate?

The idea of a health insurance mandate has seemed reasonable to many people on the right as well as the left because of the free-rider problem: those who willingly remain uninsured will have extra money to spend, and if they become sick and need care they cannot pay for, they will look to everyone else to provide that care for free. Without a mandate, are we not rewarding them for being irresponsible and allowing them to be free riders on the rest of society?

The free-rider argument seems persuasive until we ask this question: If we require everyone to have health insurance, what is the appropriate punishment for someone who avoids it? The only practical way to enforce a mandate is with a fine. But if a fine is all we need, we do not need a mandate. We need only a system that fines people who don't purchase insurance.

In fact, the income tax has long provided such a "fine." Middle-income families who have employer-provided health insurance (as opposed to higher wages) receive a generous tax break. The flip side of that tax break is a penalty: People who don't have employer-provided insurance pay higher taxes.

There is an even more important consideration with respect to the ACA: the vast majority of the uninsured are not affected by the mandate.

That's the conclusion of a new analysis by the Congressional Budget Office and the Joint Committee on Taxation, reported in the *Wall Street*

Journal.[68] According to the estimate, 90 percent of the uninsured in 2016 will be exempt from the mandate. Only 4 million people are expected to pay a fine for being uninsured that year.

The latest estimate is a substantial revision of the estimate the CBO made when the law was originally passed. In 2010, the agency estimated that about two-thirds of the uninsured would be exempt.[69] Why the substantial increase in the latest report? It appears that the Obama administration has become increasingly liberal in its willingness to let people escape because of "hardships."

Certain exemptions are written into the law itself. For example, the mandate doesn't apply to American Indians, to people who have religious objections, or to people who earn too little to be required to file an income tax return.

But the administration has piled on with fourteen ways people can avoid the fine based on hardships. These include homelessness, domestic violence, being evicted from a residence, having a utility cut off, property damage from a fire or flood, and even a canceled insurance plan.[70] Also, people can avoid the penalty if a close family member has died recently or if they have medical expenses resulting in substantial debt. People can even claim an exemption if they experienced "hardship obtaining health insurance" (couldn't negotiate HealthCare.gov). Although the government is asking for documentation to back up that claim, it doesn't require it.[71]

So if the mandate affects very few of the uninsured, who does it affect? *People who are insured.*[72]

Up to 80 percent of the people who had individual insurance last year will lose their coverage by the time all the ACA rules completely set in. Up to 90 percent of the plans that cover people at work will lose their grandfathered status.[73] In many of these cases, people are being forced to buy richer and more expensive plans—with more coverage than they want or need. In other cases, they may lose insurance altogether.

Early reports are that the trend for small business to dump their health plans and move employees onto the exchanges is occurring faster than was expected.[74] Furthermore, we can learn better ways of preventing people from gaming the system by looking at Medicare. The ACA is not the only health program in the United States that requires insurers to accept all comers, regardless of health condition, and forbids charging higher premiums to people with higher expected healthcare costs.

Medicare Part B (doctors' services), Medicare Part D (the drug benefit), and Medigap insurance are all guaranteed issue and community rated. Yet, none of these programs has a mandate. Still, they all discourage gaming. That's because in general people must sign up for them when they are eligible or face higher (and in some cases much higher) premiums when they do enroll.

For example, under Medigap in many states, a person who waits to enroll until he has a health problem can be charged a premium that reflects his true actuarial health risks—thus losing protection for preexisting conditions.

If we structure the ACA the same way, there would be no need for a mandate and no need for a great many other bureaucratic burdens.

Inviting Interference by Special Interests

Why is it good not to have a mandate? Because once the government tells us what kind of insurance coverage we must have, every special interest imaginable will lobby Congress to become part of the mandated benefit package. Special interests have been lobbying heavily at the state level for years. Insurance plans in various states are required to cover providers ranging from acupuncturists to naturopaths and services ranging from in-vitro fertilization to marriage counseling. All told, in 2010 there were 2,156 mandates at the state level.[75] These mandates have pushed up insurance premiums and priced as many as one in four uninsured people out of the market.[76]

5

Understanding Fairness

PRIOR TO THE ACA, the American method of encouraging private health insurance was largely the byproduct of a byzantine and unfair tax code that provided an income tax exclusion for health insurance benefits provided by employers, but virtually no tax break for people who purchased insurance on their own. Instead of correcting this problem, the ACA left these distortions in place and added on a new set of distortions (through tax credits offered in the health insurance exchanges).

Most uninsured people do not have access to employer-provided health insurance, purchased with pretax dollars. If they obtain insurance at all (and if they don't qualify for an ACA tax credit) they must buy it with after-tax dollars, effectively doubling the after-tax price for middle-income families. On the other hand, if they do qualify for a tax credit on the new health insurance exchange, their subsidy may be many times greater than the tax subsidy enjoyed at work by people at the same income level.

The solution to this disparity: People who obtain health insurance should receive the same tax relief, regardless of where they obtain it—at work, in the marketplace, or in a health insurance exchange.

Tax Breaks for Private Health Insurance

The tax breaks for private health insurance are substantial. For example, federal tax benefits alone total about $274 billion a year, nationwide.[77]

How much any particular individual is subsidized, however, depends on how the insurance is purchased, as well as on the family's tax bracket. If an employee works for an employer who provides health insurance as an untaxed fringe benefit instead of higher taxable wages, the employer's premium payments avoid federal, state, and local income taxes as well as payroll taxes. For a middle-income family facing a 25-percent federal income tax rate, a 15.3-percent Federal Insurance Contributions Act (FICA) tax, and a 5-percent state income tax rate, the subsidy is 45.3 percent—with government paying almost half the cost of the insurance.

To see the financial implications of these tax breaks, consider a family health insurance plan that costs $18,000 a year. The employer's choice is to spend $18,000 on (untaxed) premiums or to forgo the fringe benefit altogether and pay the employee $18,000 more in wages. In the latter case, however, the employee will receive only $9,846 in take-home pay. A different way of looking at the same issue is to ask: How much would the worker have to earn in taxable wages in order to be able to buy the same insurance after the payment of taxes? Answer: almost $32,907. So, for sacrificing $9,846 in take-home pay, the worker is able to get a benefit that he would have to earn $32,907 to be able to purchase on his own.

Generous tax breaks, therefore, undoubtedly encourage people who would otherwise have been uninsured to obtain employer-provided insurance. There are two problems with the way these tax breaks are structured.

First, the largest breaks go to people who need them least. Under the current system, families who obtain insurance through an employer obtain a tax break worth about $2,021, on the average.[78] (See Figure 5.1.) Not everyone, however, gets the average tax break. Households earning more than $150,000 per year receive an average tax break of $4,436. By contrast, those earning between $10,000 and $20,000 receive one of only about $285. One reason is that those earning higher incomes are in higher tax brackets. For example, a family in the 35-percent tax bracket gets a tax break of 35 cents for every dollar spent on health insurance. By

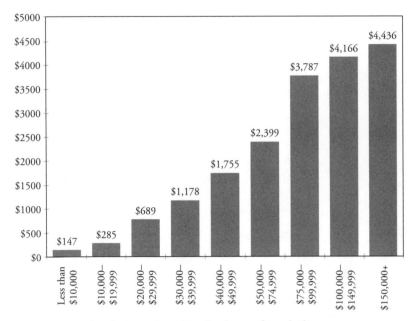

Note: Based on the Lewin Group 2011 distribution of tax subsidies.
The average tax subsidy per family is $2,021.

Figure 5.1. Average Federal Health Benefit Tax Subsidy by Family
Income Level

contrast, a family that doesn't owe any income taxes is in the 15-percent bracket (paying only the FICA payroll tax) gets a break of only 15 cents on the dollar.

Second, the people who do not obtain insurance through an employer and who do not get a subsidy in exchange get very little tax relief if they purchase insurance on their own. (See Figure 5.2.) Individuals who pay premiums with their own money can deduct costs in excess of 10 percent of adjusted gross income. For instance, an individual with $50,000 in income would not be able to deduct the first $5,000 in health insurance premiums. The threshold for someone earning $100,000 a year is twice that amount.

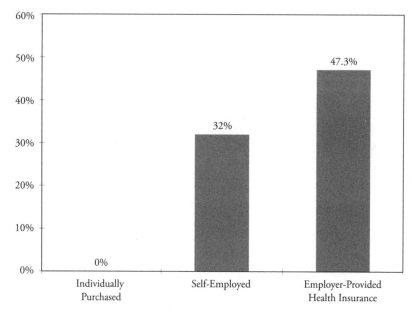

Note: Assumes taxpayer is in the 25 percent federal income tax bracket, faces a 15.3 percent payroll (FICA) tax, and a 7 percent state and local income tax.

Figure 5.2. Federal and State Tax Subsidies for Private Insurance

Individual or Group Insurance?

The difference in treatment in the tax code is not the only feature that distinguishes group insurance obtained through an employer from insurance purchased in the individual market. Employers, it is argued, are in a unique position to pool groups of people. Also, group purchase can take advantage of economies of scale. On the other hand, employer-provided insurance is not portable. People who change jobs often must also change physicians, thus losing continuity of care. Plus, there is no guarantee that insurance at the new job will provide the same coverage for the same conditions as the previous insurance policy did.

Individual insurance has the virtue of portability. People can take their coverage with them as they move from job to job. On the downside, individual insurance has higher administrative costs. But why not let employers buy individual insurance for their employees the way they currently buy group insurance? Most small employers and their employees would probably jump at the chance were it not prohibited by state laws.

The Bias toward Group Insurance

As noted, current tax law grants very generous tax breaks to middle- and upper-income employees who obtain health insurance through an employer. Yet, those same breaks are denied to individuals who purchase their own insurance. In almost everyone's estimation, this is partly the accidental result of years of tax policy rather than a methodical approach to health policy. Perhaps unintentionally, the tax-writing committees of Congress through the years have shaped and molded our health insurance system.

In many ways, the Affordable Care Act compounds the problem by introducing another arbitrary distinction. Below-average-income families get very generous tax subsidies in the health insurance exchanges that are denied to people who get health insurance at work.

Achieving Neutral Policy

In the case of individual versus group insurance, neutral policy is easy to envision and implement. A neutral government policy would give the same tax break to every form of insurance, including insurance purchased in the ACA exchanges. (See Figure 5.3) Accordingly, individual and group coverage would compete on a level playing field. In such a world, employers would not offer insurance at all unless they had a comparative advantage in doing so in their competition for labor. Undoubtedly, many large companies do have an advantage. They can do things for their employees the employees cannot do for themselves. Many small firms, however, have no such advantage and probably would be better off paying higher wages instead of paying for health insurance.

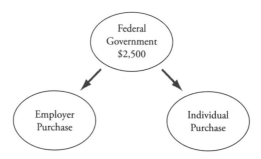

Figure 5.3. A Level Playing Field for All Insurance Policies: Goverment Subsidy for an Adult

6

Understanding
Universal Coverage

IF MAKING SURE that everyone has healthcare coverage
is a worthy goal, how can we best attempt to achieve it? We propose a
method that has so far received inadequate attention in policy circles. It
involves having the government take an amount equivalent to the total
uncollected tax subsidies and sending this money to safety-net institutions in the communities where the uninsured live. In addition, I would
allow people to use their tax credits to buy into Medicaid. Let's look at
these ideas in greater detail.

Achieving Neutrality

Suppose that the government offered every individual a uniform,
fixed-dollar subsidy. If the individual obtained private insurance, the
subsidy would be realized in the form of lower taxes by way of a tax credit.
The credit would be refundable, so that it would be available even to those
with no tax liability. If the individual chose to be uninsured, the subsidy
would be sent to a safety-net agency in the community where the person
lives. (See Figure 6.1.)

What should the amount of the credit be? As we have seen, the CBO
estimates that the cost of enrolling people in Medicaid is about $2,500
for an adult and about $8,000 for a family of four. So a credit of this
magnitude would allow people to buy Medicaid-type private health insurance. Note this is a bit more than estimates of what we are currently

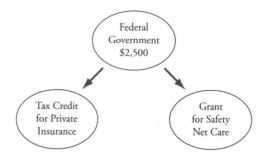

Figure 6.1. Federal Government Subsidy for an Adult

spending on free ("uncompensated") care. But if a similar amount were sent to safety net institutions for the uninsured, we would be confident that those institutions could deliver Medicaid-type care to the uninsured.

One way to think of such an arrangement is to consider it as a system in which the uninsured as a group pay for their own free care. That is, in the very act of turning down a tax credit (by choosing not to insure), uninsured individuals would pay extra taxes equal to the average amount of free care given annually to the uninsured. (See Figure 6.2.)

How can we fund the subsidies for those who choose to move from being uninsured to insured? We can do it by reversing the process. The subsidy should be funded by the reduction in expected free care that person would have consumed if uninsured. For example, suppose every adult in Dallas County, Texas, chose to obtain private insurance, relying on a refundable $2,500 federal income tax credit to pay the premiums. As

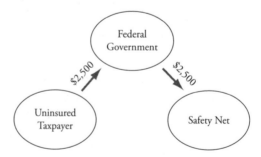

Figure 6.2. The Marginal Effect of Choosing to Be Uninsured

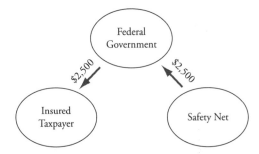

Figure 6.3. The Marginal Effect of Choosing to Be Insured

a result, Dallas County no longer would need to spend $2,500 per person on the uninsured. Thus, all of the money that previously funded safety-net medical care could be used to fund the private insurance premiums. (See Figure 6.3.)

On the other hand, if everyone in Dallas County changed their mind and opted to be uninsured, the $2,500 per person in unclaimed credits would be available for safety-net institutions.

Implementing Reform

To implement such a program, all the federal government needs to know is how many people live in each community. In principle, it will be offering each adult citizen an annual $2,500 tax credit (and each child a $1,500 credit). Some will claim the full credit. Some will claim a partial credit (because they will be insured for only part of a year). Others will claim no credit. What the government pledges to each community will be $2,500 times the number of adults who live there. The portion of this sum that is not claimed on tax returns should be available as block grants to be spent on indigent care at the local level.

The Cost of Reform

Where would the federal government get the money to fund the private insurance tax credits?

We could begin with the $300 billion in tax subsidies the federal government already "spends" to subsidize private insurance. Add to that the money the federal, state, and local governments already spend on indigent care. Then there is the $200 billion a year the federal government plans to spend on the ACA subsidies over the next ten years. That amount alone should be more than enough to finance the subsidies considered here plus a generous contribution to a Health Savings Account. And as some ACA revenues come from taxes that are especially unfair and damaging economically, we should seek to eliminate taxes on capital and businesses and replace the revenue and/or cut spending in other ways.

But we should also consider making certain tax benefits conditional on proof of insurance. For example, the $1,000 child tax credit could be made conditional on proof of insurance for a child.[79] For middle-income families, a portion of the standard deduction could be made conditional on proof of insurance for adults. For lower-income families, part of the Earned Income Tax Credit (EITC) refund could be conditional.

How would the federal government reduce safety-net spending when uninsured people elected to obtain private insurance? Because much of the safety-net expenditure already consists of federal funds, the federal government could use its share to fund private insurance tax credits instead. For the remainder, the federal government does not have direct control over the budgets of state and local governments. However, the federal government could reduce block grants to the states for Medicaid and other programs instead.

Public or Private Coverage?

Many poor and near-poor families have a choice of public or private insurance. Because of their low income, they can qualify for either Medicaid or the state-based Children's Health Insurance Program (CHIP) or obtain private insurance (typically through an employer). Clearly, we should not be indifferent about this choice. Private insurance means people are paying their own way. Further, as noted, private insurance often means better healthcare.

How does government policy affect this choice? Unfortunately, public policy overwhelmingly encourages people to drop private insurance and enroll in public programs instead. As noted, tax subsidies for employer-provided insurance are quite meager for those with near-poverty incomes (basically consisting of the avoidance of the 15.3-percent FICA tax) and nonexistent if the insurance is purchased individually. By contrast, public programs are "free." Further, except for a few pilot programs under way, states do not allow Medicaid enrollees to use their Medicaid dollars to buy into an employer plan or purchase private insurance directly.

Consequences of Perverse Incentives

Many people assume that Medicaid insures people who otherwise would not have access to private insurance. However, Medicaid induces some people to turn down or drop private coverage to take advantage of free health insurance offered by the state. As a result of such "crowding out," the cost of expanding public insurance programs has been high relative to the gain. For example, if for each new enrollee in a public program at least one person loses private insurance, there will be no net reduction in the number of uninsured, despite the higher taxpayer burden.

Economists David Cutler and Jonathan Gruber found that Medicaid expansions in the early 1990s were substantially offset by reductions in private coverage. For every additional dollar spent on Medicaid, private-sector healthcare spending was reduced by 50 cents to 75 cents, on the average.[80] Thus, taxpayers incurred a considerable burden, but at least half and perhaps as much as three-fourths of the expenditures replaced private-sector spending rather than buying more or better medical care.

A similar principle applies to the Children's Health Insurance Program (CHIP). Take a low-income working family covered by an employer-sponsored health plan. The employer might have covered some or all of the cost of insurance premiums for the employee and family with pretax dollars. However, a bigger paycheck is more attractive to actual and potential employees if coverage is provided by the state. Thus, CHIP offers some employees the opportunity to increase wages and reduce their health insurance costs.

Overall, the proportion of poor children without health insurance fell from 19 percent in 1997 to 11 percent in 2003. During this period, the percentage of low-income children enrolled in public programs increased from 29 percent to 49 percent. At the same time, private insurance coverage fell from 47 percent to 35 percent, although there was little change in the percentage of privately insured children in households at higher income levels. It appears that the crowd-out of private insurance caused by the expansion of public programs was about 60 percent.[81]

Adopting a Policy of Neutrality

The solution here is very similar to the solution to the previous problem. If government is spending $2,500 a year per adult enrolled in Medicaid, it ought to be willing to spend an identical sum on private insurance instead. (See Figure 6.4.)

On paper, Medicaid coverage often looks more generous than private insurance—covering almost all physicians, facilities, and procedures at no out-of-pocket cost to the patient, at least in principle. In practice, many physicians refuse to see Medicaid patients and, because of the low rates of reimbursement, care is often rationed by waiting. As a result, a policy that is financially neutral would be one that encourages private insurance.

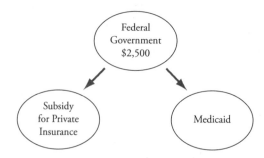

Figure 6.4. A Level Playing field for Private and Public Insurance: Government Subsidy for an Adult

7

Understanding Portability

ONE OF THE biggest problems with the U.S. healthcare system is that health insurance obtained through an employer is usually not portable. In general, when you leave your employer, you must eventually lose the health insurance plan your employer was providing. Almost all of the problems people have with preexisting conditions arise because of a transition from employer-provided insurance to individually purchased insurance. And those problems arise because the employee doesn't own the insurance the employer provides.

Insurance obtained in the (ACA) health insurance exchange is also not generally portable. For example, people lose their eligibility for insurance purchased in an exchange (or lose their eligibility for tax-subsidized insurance) if they become eligible for Medicaid or if they accept a job with an employer who provides minimum essential coverage for an affordable price.

The case for portability is strong. First, portability allows a long-lasting relationship with a health plan, which in turn allows a long-lasting relationship with providers of care. This means that people who switch jobs frequently can still have continuity of care—which is usually a prerequisite for high-quality care. Second, people who have portable insurance (as well as portable retirement plans and other benefits) will not be locked into jobs solely because of the non-portable nature of their benefits. Portable benefits are consistent with a mobile labor market, which is a necessary component of a dynamic, competitive economy. Finally, a system of portable benefits is one in which the employer's role is financial, rather than administrative. Employers, therefore, can specialize in what they do best, leaving health insurance to firms that specialize in the business of insurance.

Freeing the Employee

Public opinion polls show that portable insurance—insurance that travels with the employee from job to job and in and out of the labor market—is highly popular. So if everyone wants portable insurance, why don't we have it?

First, as we have seen, the federal tax law generously subsidizes employer-provided insurance, but it offers very little tax relief to those who must purchase insurance on their own. One big exception to that generalization is the health insurance exchange, where people whose income is below 400 percent of the federal poverty level are entitled to subsidies in the form of tax credits.

Outside the exchanges, employer-paid premiums avoid federal income taxes, federal payroll taxes (FICA), and state and local income taxes as well. But individuals tend to get none of these tax benefits when they pay premiums on their own.

Even with these discriminatory tax subsidies, insurance could still be portable if employers bought individually owned insurance rather than group insurance for their employees. But here is the second problem. It is illegal in almost every state for employers to use pretax dollars to purchase individually owned insurance. And the Obama administration has ruled that employers also cannot use pretax dollars to purchase employee-owned insurance in the health insurance exchanges. If they do they will face very large fines.

Both state and federal laws need to change. We need to move in the opposite direction—making it as easy as possible for employees to obtain portable health insurance.

Freeing the Employer

When health insurance is company specific, the employer is necessarily involved in the management and administration of every employee's healthcare. Manufacturers of automobiles, for example, find that they are in the health insurance business as well as the car manufacturing business. Ditto for the makers of home appliances, electronic equipment, and every other good or service in our economy. Most employers, and certainly all small-business owners, would prefer not to be in the health insurance business, however. In a world of portable insurance, they would not have to be.

Rather than offering health insurance as a defined benefit, employers should be able to offer health insurance as a defined contribution. They would make a monetary contribution to the health insurance premiums of each employee, each pay period. The 401(k) retirement plan is a model. New employees would know not only their salary, but also how much the employer is willing to pay toward the cost of insurance. In this way, the employer's role in health insurance is purely financial. In fact, employers would have no more involvement in the employee's health plans than they have in their employee's 401(k) portfolio.

Freeing the Nontraditional Workplace

If a new employee has coverage under a spouse's health plan, he or she doesn't need duplicate coverage. But the laws governing the workplace do not allow the employer to pay higher wages instead.[82] On the other hand, a part-time employee might be willing to accept lower wages in return for the opportunity to enroll in the employer's health plan. Yet, the law does not allow that either.

The institutional structures of our tax system and our employee benefits system were formed decades ago when lawmakers had a simple view of how life would be lived: There would be a full-time worker husband and a homemaker wife who, if she entered the labor market at all, would do so only temporarily. If this is the way you live your life, these institutions will still work pretty well for you. But many people don't these days.

To bring our labor market institutions into the twenty-first century, employers should be free to give employees the option to choose between nontaxed benefits and taxable wages, where appropriate.

8

Understanding Patient Power

WHO SHOULD CONTROL the healthcare purse strings? It turns out that most of the time the system works well when patients are in control—directing the spending and weighing the tradeoffs between healthcare and other uses of money.

How Patients Make Their Own Choices between Healthcare and Other Uses of Money

The classic investigation of this issue was conducted by the RAND Corporation about 30 years ago.[83] In that study:

People with a deductible of about $2,500 (in today's prices) cut back on spending by about 30 percent relative to people who faced no out-of-pocket healthcare costs.

Essentially, the higher deductible had no negative impact on health. People with high deductibles were as likely to cut back on useful health services as they were to cut back on unnecessary care, however.[84]

Latter-day critics seized on the last finding to argue that patient choices appear to be random, and therefore the experiment in consumer-directed care showed it to be a failure. In fact, the patients' behavior is exactly what you would expect from a rational consumer of any product. When something is free, the temptation is to take everything that is offered. The incentive to distinguish between what is "necessary" or "useful" and "unnecessary" or "un-useful" is largely nonexistent. When you have to pay market prices, however, you have an incentive to pay more attention—figuring out what's unnecessary or of marginal value.

In the thirty-year period since the RAND experiment was conducted, a number of experiments—both within the United States and abroad—have explored ways to create greater patient cost-sharing without encouraging people to forgo needed care. These include Medisave Accounts in Singapore[85] (dating from 1984), Medical Savings Accounts in South Africa[86] (dating from 1993); and in the United States, an MSA pilot program[87](dating from 1996), the current Health Savings Account program[88] (dating from 2004), Health Reimbursement Arrangements[89] (dating from 2002), and even cash accounts in Medicaid.[90] Many of these experiments have been subjected to considerable academic scrutiny.

Virtually every serious study of consumer-directed healthcare has reached conclusions similar to the original RAND research. One of the most comprehensive of those (but not as comprehensive as the original) was conducted by RAND itself. It concluded that people with high-deductible plans and HSAs spend about 30 percent less on healthcare than those with conventional coverage, with no apparent adverse effects on health.[91]

Interestingly, the latest RAND study gave special attention to the plight of "vulnerable families" (low-income and/or high-risk). The finding: These patients are not disadvantaged by the spending reductions. The researchers report:

> There are no statistically significant differences between non-vulnerable families and low-income or high-risk families in terms of dollar reductions in total spending that result from benefit designs and few differences in the components of spending. How-

ever, since high-risk families have higher levels of spending, the proportional reductions in total annual spending are generally smaller for those at high risk.[92]

RAND researchers were particularly concerned about whether vulnerable families would fail to receive recommended preventive care services. They found:

> As with spending, there are few significant differences between low-income and non-vulnerable families regarding the effect of plan design on receipt of the cancer screening. However, there are significant differences for those at high risk. For them, a high deductible is not associated with reductions in receipt of two of the three recommended procedures, and the reduction for the third is significantly less than for the non-vulnerable population, though this latter is not significant when we adjust for multiple comparisons.[93]

In other words, people at high risk are not deterred by the plan design from getting screening.

How the Supply Side Responds

The biggest change brought about by giving patients direct control over healthcare dollars is not on the demand side of the market. It's on the supply side. Here are some examples of healthcare markets dominated by patients paying out-of-pocket for services.

Cosmetic Surgery[94]

Cosmetic surgery is rarely covered by insurance. Because providers know their patients must pay out of pocket and are price-sensitive, patients can typically (1) find a package price in advance covering all services and facilities, (2) compare prices prior to surgery, and (3) pay a price that has been falling over time in real terms—despite a huge increase in volume and considerable technical innovation (which is blamed for increasing costs for every other type of surgery).

Laser Eye Surgery[95]

Competition is also holding prices in check for vision correction surgery, and laser eye surgeons compete on quality as well. Recent quality improvements include more accurate correction, faster healing, fewer side effects, and an expanded range of patients and conditions that can be treated. For instance, rather than traditional LASIK surgery, patients can pay slightly more per eye for the newer, wavefront-guided LASIK.

Laboratory and Diagnostic Testing[96]

Patients can order their own blood tests without a doctor's appointment and compare prices at different diagnostic testing facilities. Prices are 50 percent to 80 percent lower than identical tests performed in a hospital setting. These services lower patients' time costs as well as money costs. In many cases, the results are available online within 24 to 48 hours.

Price Competition for Drugs[97]

Wal-mart became the first nationwide retailer to compete aggressively for buyers of generic drugs by charging a low, uniform price—$10 for a ninety-day supply. In many cases, patients with drug coverage have found the cash price at Wal-mart to be lower than their health plan's copay at conventional pharmacies. Some chain drugstores have responded with their own pricing strategies.

Price Competition for Drugs over the Internet[98]

Rx.com was the first mail-order pharmacy to compete online in a national market for drugs. To compete with local pharmacies, they offer lower costs and more convenient service, including free home delivery. They also compete on quality. For instance, high-volume mail-order pharmacies have much lower dispensing error rates than conventional pharmacies. Online mail-order pharmacies have thrived on the business model of improved quality, lower cost, and greater convenience.

Patient Education for Drugs as a Product[99]

DestinationRx.com is a pharmacy benefits management company. In addition to operating an online mail-order drug delivery service, it also offers a website to help patients identify low-cost therapeutic substitutes for the drugs they currently take. In addition, the firm is partnering with Safeway supermarkets to install drug comparison kiosks in store pharmacies.

Retail Clinics[100]

Walk-in clinics in shopping malls and drugstores offer primary care services. They compete by offering low costs in terms of both time and money. To ensure a consistent level of quality, nurse practitioners follow computerized protocols, and electronic medical records are a natural adjunct of that process. Furthermore, once such a system is in place, electronic prescriptions are a straightforward next step, and electronic prescribing allows the use of error-reducing software. One study found that MinuteClinics follow treatment guidelines better than traditional medical practices.[101]

Telephone-Based Practices [102]

As of April 2014, Teladoc has 7.5 million customers paying for a telephone consultation—access to a doctor at any time of day from any location. And because each on-call physician needs access to patients' medical histories (and the treatment decisions of previous physicians), personal and portable electronic medical records are a necessary part of the company's business model. The physicians prescribe drugs electronically—facilitating the use of safety-enhancing software that checks for harmful interactions.

Concierge Medical Practices [103]

Some innovative physicians are rebundling and repricing medical services in ways that are not possible under third-party insurance. For a fixed monthly fee, they offer same-day or next-day appointments, help in scheduling diagnostic tests and appointments with specialists, help in negotiating prices and fees, and other services. Many will meet their patients at the emergency room to ensure prompt service.

Concierge physicians tend to relate to their patients in much the same way lawyers, accountants, engineers, and other professionals interact with their clients—including phone calls, email consultations, and convenient Web-based services.

Concierge Services for Patients with High Deductibles

You don't actually have to leave your health insurance plan to take advantage of concierge doctor services. Compass of Dallas is a firm that specializes in helping people with high-deductible insurance wade through the complexities of the medical marketplace. For example, the company "will search for the least expensive hospital or facility for a given procedure, find doctors who best suit a patient's wants and needs, screen for best outcomes and the fewest lawsuits, set up appointments, make sense of bills, and challenge questionable ones."[104]

"If we find mistakes, which by the way happens quite a bit, we can go back and speak the same coding language with the doctor's office or hospital and say, 'Let's reevaluate this and see if it needs to be coded differently and resubmitted,'" says Eric Bricker, the company's CEO. "We might find three in-network primary care physicians who take same-day or next-day appointments and are within their geographic area."[105]

The Ideal Medical Savings Account

As good as Health Savings Accounts are, the current structure is not ideal. Consider people in the 25-percent income tax bracket. If they take a dollar out of an HSA and spend it on other goods and services, they must pay 25 cents in taxes. If they are not yet 65 years of age, there will be another 20 percent penalty, leaving them with only 55 cents for other spending. For this person, a dollar's worth of healthcare trades against 55 cents of other goods and services.

As Mark Pauly and I explained in *Health Affairs* some time ago, an ideal account is one that does not distort incentives.[106] In the current period, people must choose between spending on healthcare and spending on other goods and services. When saving comes into play, people must choose between current and future healthcare and between future healthcare and future other goods and services. An ideal savings account is one that keeps all these choices on a level playing field with respect to the tax law.

I call this account a Roth Health Savings Account, or Roth HSA. The Roth account involves after-tax deposits and tax-free withdrawals. That means a dollar of healthcare always trades on a level playing field against every other use to which that dollar can be put—both in the current period and in future periods. This is the account that is most compatible with subsidizing health insurance with lump-sum tax credits and it is the approach actually used in the health insurance. It is also the approach advocated more generally by Sen. John McCain[107] in his 2008 election bid and is incorporated in the Coburn/Burr/Ryan/Nunes health reform bill.[108] This type of account would also be ideal for reforming Medicare.

Implications for HSA Design

The left side of Figure 8.1 illustrates the design of HSAs in employer plans as mandated by federal law.[109] In this example, the plan pays all costs above a deductible of $3,000 (with the exception of preventive care). The HSA deposit in this example is $2,000. Thus, the employee pays the first $2,000 of medical expenses from the HSA and the next $1,000 is paid out of pocket. Any remaining costs are paid by the plan.

(Note that with freedom comes added responsibility. In current employer plans, individuals are usually free to use their HSA funds to purchase non-covered services. So, an employee might spend all of his or her HSA account on chiropractor services—even if these services are not covered by the plan and the payments do not count toward the deductible. A careless employee could exhaust the HSA funds on non-covered services and risk having to pay the entire deductible out of pocket.)

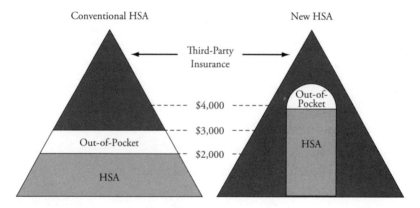

Figure 8.1

However, HSAs designed in this way are not necessarily ideal. The design pictured on the right side of Figure 8.1 is preferable. Under this design, the plan pays first dollar for some treatments, while leaving the insured free to pay even higher amounts for other services.

The diagram on the right has become a reality in South Africa. In 1993, virtually all major forms of insurance in that country began competing on a level playing field (HMOs, PPOs, etc.), partly owing to liberal insurance regulations and partly to a favorable ruling from the South African equivalent of our Internal Revenue Service. Anyone with an idea on how to design a better health insurance plan was free to try. And during the decade of the 1990s, Medical Savings Account (MSA) plans captured more than half of the market for private health insurance.[110]

Under U.S. law, a tax-free HSA for Americans must have at least a $1,250 for 2014 deductible for individuals and $2,500 for families. And the deductible applies to all services other than preventive care. South African MSAs are more flexible. The typical plan there has first-dollar insurance coverage for most hospital procedures—on the theory that within hospitals, patients have little opportunity to exercise choices. On the other hand, a high deductible applies to discretionary expenses, including most services delivered in doctors' offices.[111]

South Africa's more flexible approach also allows more sensible drug coverage. While the high deductible applies to most drugs for ordinary patients, a typical plan pays from the first dollar for drugs that treat diabetes, asthma, and other chronic conditions. The theory: It's not smart to encourage patients to skimp on drugs that prevent more-expensive-to-treat conditions from developing.[112]

9

Understanding Real Insurance

The Design of Third-Party Payment

MOST EMPLOYER PLANS these days allow employees to seek care "out of network" by paying a higher copayment. This option has been popular because employees complained about the restrictiveness of closed networks. Yet, analysts say that such options can raise the cost of health insurance substantially.[113] It seems that people flock to managed care plans to take advantage of their low premiums, then demand options that undermine the ability of the plans to keep costs down.

The approach summarized in Table 9.1 points to a partial solution. The reason out-of-network doctors cost more, even when paid the same fees as in-network physicians, is that they are likely to order more tests and generate the use of more ancillary services. But this would be of much

Table 9.1. General Rules

Individual Choice	Collective Choice
1. No risky medical event	1. Risky medical event
2. Price of third-party insurance is high	2. Price of third-party insurance is low
3. Exercise of choice creates no externalities	3. Exercise of choice creates risks for others

less concern if third-party payments were restricted largely to treatment or curative services and patients paid with their HSA funds for diagnostic services.

The problem remains of how to control curative costs without unduly restricting patient choice or endangering quality. A possible solution is a variant on an old idea: a fee schedule. From time to time, the insurance industry has flirted with plans that pay doctors a set fee for various services. If patients selected doctors who charge more, they paid the difference out of pocket. In modern medicine, we know that the doctor's fee is only one part of a complex array of costs a doctor can generate. So controlling the physician's fee isn't enough. But why not fix the plan's cost for an entire treatment regimen?

Some commentators refer to insurance designed in this way as "value-based" health insurance[114] or "reference pricing."[115] However, it is also consistent with some of the characteristics of traditional casualty insurance.

Suppose a patient is diagnosed with cancer, and the health plan normally would contract to pay a fixed fee to a medical facility to cover all costs. If the plan could be assured that this fixed fee were its maximum exposure, the plan would have no economic interest in restricting the patient's choices. It could, for example, allow the patient to go to an alternative provider and pay more, if needed, out of pocket or from an HSA. In this way, the plan controls its costs, and patients still exercise choice. Also, the exercise of choice puts pressure on the plan to maintain quality in its own preferred medical facility.

The decision to take the plan's money and seek treatment elsewhere need not be made once and for all. For chronic conditions, it could be reaffirmed annually. Take diabetes. Because traditional care for diabetes has been less than optimal, many patients and doctors have long maintained that patients (with the help of a physician) can manage diabetes more efficiently than managed care can.[116] Why not let them try? The health plan might make an annual deposit to the patient's HSA and shift the entire year's financial responsibility to the patient. If there were concerns that the funds might be wasted, the health plan could hold the account and monitor it.

An example of the range of possibilities is again provided by South Africa. Discovery Health (one of the largest sellers of MSA plans there) allows its diabetic patients the opportunity to enroll in a special diabetes management program. Under the arrangement, Discovery pays the program about $75 per month, while patients pay another $25 from their MSA accounts. Discovery is considering handling many other chronic diseases in the same way.[117]

Here are a few other examples, closer to home. Wal-mart has selected seven centers of excellence for elective surgery. Employees can go to other providers, but they may face out-of-pocket charges of $5,000 or $6,000. Lowe's has a similar arrangement with the Cleveland Clinic for cardiac surgery. This is what I call "domestic medical tourism." I like it. But it's not the only approach. Safeway, the national grocery store chain, has established a reference price for 451 laboratory tests—set at about the 60th percentile (60 percent of the facilities charge this price or less). If the employees choose a more expensive facility, they must pay the extra cost out of their own pockets.

Case Study: Joint Replacements in California

Lab tests are relatively inexpensive. How well would reference pricing work for big ticket items? WellPoint, operating in California as Anthem Blue Cross, started with joint replacements and the results are fascinating. They are planning to extend the approach to as many as 900 additional procedures this year.

Like other third-party payers, WellPoint discovered that the charges for hip and knee replacements in California were all over the map, ranging from $15,000 to $110,000. Yet, there were forty-six hospitals that routinely averaged $30,000 or less. So WellPoint entered an agreement with CalPERS (the health plan for California state employees, retirees, and their families) to pay for these procedures in a different way. WellPoint created a type of network (I have been informed that this is not technically a "network," but I'm going to call it that anyway) consisting of the forty-six facilities. There was no special negotiation with these hospitals, however.

WellPoint simply encouraged their enrollees to go to there. Patients were free to go to elsewhere, but they were told in advance that WellPoint would pay no more than $30,000 for a joint replacement outside the network. (At all the hospitals, patients pay a 20 percent copayment up to $3,000.)

Take a look at Figure 9.1. The patients in this graph have been adjusted for case severity and geographical diversity in a study by Berkeley health economist James Robinson and his colleague Timothy Brown.[118] The bottom two lines show patients who went to the forty-six hospitals. The light gray line reflects the average cost for CalPERS patients who, beginning in

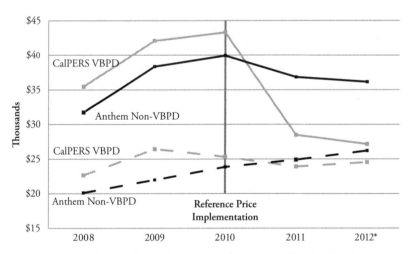

Source: California Public Employees Retirement System (CalPERS) and Anthem Blue Cross. All prices in 2011 dollars. VBPD: Value Based Purchasing Design. *Through September of 2012 only.

Figure 9.1. Prices for Knee and Hip Replacement Surgery in California Hospitals before and after the Implementation of Reference Pricing

2010, were enrolled in WellPoint's new program. The black line is the control group. As the figure shows, there is not that much difference between the two populations in terms of the cost of their procedures.

Now look at the top two lines. The light gray line represents the average cost for CalPERS patients who went outside the network (about 30 percent of the total). Beginning in 2010, they undoubtedly told the providers they had only $30,000 to spend. As the figure shows, the cost of care at these hospitals was cut by one-third in the first year and continued heading toward the average "network" price over the next two years.

This is dramatic evidence that when patients are responsible for the marginal cost of their care (and therefore, providers have to compete on price) healthcare markets become competitive very quickly. Remember, the insurer is not bargaining with these out-of-network providers. The patients are.

Look at the uppermost black line. These are (control group) patients who are not telling providers they have only $30,000 to spend. Nonetheless, their price/cost of care begins declining in 2010 as well. This is exactly what would happen in the market for canned corn or for loaves of bread. People who comparison shop affect the price paid by those who don't.

Now ask yourself this very important question: Who is more powerful at controlling healthcare costs? Huge third-party bureaucracies negotiating with providers? Or patients paying the marginal cost of their care?

The Casualty Insurance Model

After an automobile accident, a claims adjuster inspects the damage, agrees on a price, and writes the car owner a check. Hail damage to a home's roof is handled in the same way under a homeowner's policy. In both cases, the insured is free to make decisions about paying for damage repair. In contrast, traditional health insurance is based on the idea that insurers should pay not for conditions, but for medical care. That health insurers rejected the casualty model is not surprising. Blue Cross was started by hospitals for the purpose of insuring that hospital bills would be paid. Blue Shield was started by doctors to ensure that doctor fees would be paid.[119] Had auto insurance been developed by auto repair shops, they also would have rejected the casualty model.

I am not suggesting that we give the insured complete freedom of choice. Paying people for a condition and allowing them to forgo health-care and spend the money on pleasure may not be in the self-interest of a health insurance pool because an untreated condition today could develop into a new and more expensive-to-treat condition later on.[120] I am suggesting that if people were largely free to make their own treatment choices and the market were free to meet their needs, health insurance would take a major step in the direction of the casualty model.

Covered Services

One of the most contentious issues in health policy today concerns the services health insurers must cover. Special interests have persuaded state legislatures and Congress to require insurers to cover a vast array of costly services, whether or not those buying the insurance want to pay for the coverage.[121]

Traditional insurance has made a lot of arbitrary distinctions that an ideal plan need not make. For example, traditional insurance pays for treatment of back problems by a doctor of medicine, but not a chiropractor. It pays for mental health services provided by a psychiatrist, but not a psychologist. The rationale was partly a misplaced attempt to save money, but it also reflected the physicians' interest in promoting insurance that pays for the services of doctors rather than the patient's interest in protecting against catastrophic costs.

The casualty model of insurance helps solve this problem. Health plans could control costs and give patients greater freedom to choose among competing providers at the same time. Coupled with the idea that people should pay their full cost when entering a health plan and that medical consumption decisions not arising from a risky event should be paid by the individual from an HSA, our ideal health plan should make coverage decisions a lot easier.

Terms of Exit

Recall that (pre–ACA) insurance contracts in the individual market were almost always guaranteed to be renewable. Once in an insurance pool, people were entitled to remain there indefinitely and pay the same premiums others pay, regardless of changes in their health status. That commitment was completely one-sided, however. The insurer made an indefinite commitment to the members, but the members were free to leave the pool at any time.

This one-way commitment created the following problem. New insurance pools attracted mainly healthy people because insurers tended to deny coverage to, or attach exclusions and riders limiting the coverage of, people who were already sick (the result of a process known as *medical underwriting*). As time passed, some enrollees got sick, and the premium paid by all needed to be increased to cover the cost of their care. Thus, mature insurance pools (ones that have been around longer) almost always charged higher premiums than young pools. This gave healthy people an incentive to leave the mature pool. By switching to a young pool, healthy people could escape high premiums. But this option was not open to the sick members of the mature pool. If they tried to switch, the new pool would either deny them coverage or charge them a higher premium because of their medical condition. As a result, it was not unusual in the individual market to find an insurer providing the same coverage, but charging vastly different premiums, depending on the age of the pool. Members of a mature pool, for example, might pay $1,000 a month or more for their coverage, while entrants into a young pool might pay only a few hundred dollars. Clearly, these are not the features of an ideal insurance system.

One possible solution is to make the long-term commitment apply both ways. In return for an indefinite commitment on the part of the insurer, members would commit to the pool for a defined period—for example, three, four, or five years. This does not mean that people would remain stuck in a plan they wished to leave. It does mean that leaving the pool would require the consent of the pool. For example, if a healthy member left high-cost plan A to join low-cost plan B, B would compensate A for its loss. Conversely, if a sick member left A to join B, A would compensate B to take the member and pay for the higher expected cost of care.[122] In this model, re-contracting is always possible, but only the type of re-contracting that leaves everybody better off.[123]

Moreover, in the ideal system described here, people would have far less reason to switch insurers because their pool would be providing mainly financial (insurance) services rather than healthcare. A member would not need to switch from plan A to plan B to see a particular doctor or gain a higher quality of care.

Getting from Here to There: Deregulating the Exchanges

Right now the individual market is being replaced with health insurance that is bought and sold in highly regulated exchanges. Rather than seeking to abolish these institutions, might they be deregulated and denationalized in order to create a genuinely free market?

Exchanges without Mandates

The first things that need to go are the individual and employer mandates. As far as getting people insured, the employer mandate appears to have a negligible effect anyway, and it's very bad for the job market.[124] Even the individual mandate is expected to affect only about 10 percent of the uninsured, according to the latest estimates of the Congressional Budget Office and the Joint Committee on Taxation.[125] And under the best estimates, most of the uninsured will still be uninsured after the ACA is fully phased in.[126]

Plus the mandate forces people to buy a product designed by politicians, rather than one that meets individual and family needs. And as we have seen, we don't need mandates in order to keep people from gaming the system. We have found better ways in Medicare Part B, Medicare Part D and with Medigap. In those markets, if you don't buy when you are eligible, you can face penalties.

Exchanges without Artificial Prices

As previously noted, the ACA regulations are inducing insurers to choose narrow networks in order to keep costs down and premiums low.[127] They are doing that on the theory that only sick people pay attention to networks and the healthy buy on price; and they are clearly trying to attract the healthy and avoid the sick. The perverse incentives that are causing these perverse results have one and only one cause: when individuals enter a health plan, the premium the insurer receives is different from the enrollee's expected medical costs.

Precisely the opposite happens in the Medicare Advantage program, where Medicare makes a significant effort to pay insurers actuarially fair premiums. The enrollees themselves all pay the same premium, but Medicare adds an additional sum, depending on the enrollee's expected costs. For example, some special needs plans are paid as much as $60,000 or more, per enrollee. Under this system, all enrollees are financially attractive to insurers, regardless of health status.

Exchanges without Government Risk Adjustment

What we call "change of health status insurance" would begin with the Medicare Advantage risk adjustment formulas.[128] However, the extra premium adjustments would be paid by insurers to each other—not by

Medicare. Further, the insurers would be able to improve on Medicare's formulas as they learn of better methods of adjustment. They would also be able to use "look back" techniques to adjust the payments through time, when they discover the original estimated expense was too high or too low. The risk adjustment we are describing here is adjustment produced by the marketplace, not by a bureaucracy.

Exchanges without Limited Enrollment Periods

Almost no one in the United States could buy health insurance after the March 31 deadline except in those states where the deadline was extended. The only exceptions were for a qualifying event (divorce, loss of a job, etc.). The next opportunity was on November 15, and even then they could only buy insurance that became effective on January 1, 2015.[129] These limited enrollment periods exist in order to keep people from switching plans as their health condition changes. And the reason that is viewed as undesirable is that people would take advantage of the system—paying low premiums for skimpy coverage when they are healthy and then choosing a rich plan after they need serious medical care.

But it is actually good for people to switch plans after they get sick. Don't we want to fit the right plan to the right patient when health conditions change? The only reason plan switching is viewed as a problem is because none of the premiums are actuarially fair. In a rational insurance market, people would be able to continuously move from plan to plan. But they would have to pay the full actuarially fair price of any upgrade and they would receive the full actuarially fair discount for any downgrade.

PART III

Curing the Healthcare Crisis

10

Can the ACA Be Fixed?

IT'S A 2,700-PAGE bill. There are 20,000 pages of regulations. Major provisions seem to change every other week. And despite Nancy Pelosi's promise, four years after it passed most of us still aren't sure about everything that's in it. How can something like that possibly be fixed?

It's easier than you might suppose. Here are four simple reforms that would solve many of the problems caused by the ACA:

- Replace all the ACA mandates and subsidies with a universal tax credit that is the same for everyone.
- Replace all the different types of medical savings accounts with a Roth Health Savings Account (after-tax deposits and tax-free withdrawals).
- Allow Medicaid to compete with private insurance, with everyone having the right to buy in or get out.
- Denationalize and deregulate the exchanges and require them to institute change-of-health-status insurance.

Clearly much more needs to be done. But you could keep an awful lot of the ACA and still have a workable healthcare system by making these changes and these changes alone.

Let me describe all of the mechanical problems that would be solved with these changes. Then I will show that these changes would also get all the important economic incentives right.

Technical Problems with the Online Exchanges Would Be Gone

Virtually every problem with the online exchanges has one and only one cause: People at different income levels and in different insurance pools get different subsidies from the federal government.

Consider that when you apply for insurance on an exchange, the exchange has to check with the IRS to verify your income; it needs to check with Social Security to see how many different employers you work for; it needs to check with the Department of Labor to see if those employers are offering affordable, qualified insurance; and it has to check with your state Medicaid program to see if you are eligible for that.

To make matters worse, the subsidy you get this year is almost certain to be the wrong amount. Whether people use last year's income or guess what this year's will be, they are almost certain to err. If they underestimate what they will earn, their subsidy will be too high, and they will have to give money back to the IRS next April 15. If they overestimate, their subsidy will be too low, and they will be entitled to a refund. All of this will be annoying. It may also cause financial hardship.

With a universal tax credit, it doesn't matter where you work or what your employer offers you. It doesn't matter what your income is. It doesn't matter if you qualify for Medicaid. You get the same subsidy regardless of any of those things.

That means that we could turn all of the exchanges over to EHealth, which has been operating an online private exchange for a decade and has insured more than 4 million people.

All Perverse Outcomes in the
Labor Market Would Be Gone

As we have seen, under the ACA, employers have perverse incentives to keep the number of employees small, to reduce their hours of work, to use independent contractors and temp labor instead of full-time employees, to end insurance for below average-wage employees, to self-insure while the workforce is healthy, and pay fines instead of providing full insurance if they become unhealthy.

With a universal tax credit and no mandate, all of these perversions would evaporate. The subsidy for private health insurance would be the same for all: whether they work on the assembly line or whether they are a CEO; whether they work less or more than 30 hours a week; whether their workplace has fewer or more than fifty employees; whether they are in a union or not; and whether their employer provides the insurance or whether they obtain it on their own.

The "Race to the Bottom" in the Health
Insurance Exchanges Would End

There are three main features of insurance: a benefit package, a network of providers, and a premium.[130] The ACA regulations fix the benefit package and leave insurers free to compete on networks and premiums. Insurers are responding by choosing narrow networks to keep costs down and premiums low.[131] They are doing that on the theory that only sick people pay attention to networks and the healthy buy on price; and they are clearly trying to attract the healthy and avoid the sick.

The perverse incentives that are causing these counterproductive results have one and only one cause: When individuals enter a health plan, the premium the insurer receives is different from the enrollee's expected medical costs.

Precisely the opposite happens in the Medicare Advantage program, where Medicare makes a significant effort to pay insurers an actuarially fair premium. The enrollees themselves all pay the same premium, but Medicare adds an additional sum, depending on the enrollee's expected costs. For example, some special-needs plans are paid as much as $60,000 per enrollee. Under this system, all enrollees are financially attractive to insurers, regardless of health status.

What we are calling "change of health status insurance" would accomplish the same result.[132] The only difference is that the extra premium adjustments would be paid by one insurer to another, and the amount paid would be determined in the marketplace—not by Medicare.

People Would No Longer Be Trapped in One Insurance System Rather Than Another

Under the ACA, if you are offered affordable coverage by an employer, you are not allowed to buy subsidized insurance in the exchange. If you are a dependent of an employee who is offered affordable individual coverage, you are not allowed to buy subsidized insurance in the exchange, even if the coverage offered to you is not affordable. If you are eligible for Medicaid, you are not allowed into the exchange. If your income is below 100 percent of the federal poverty level, you are not allowed into the exchange, even if you aren't eligible for Medicaid.

To make matters worse, eligibility for one system versus another will change frequently for millions of people because of fluctuations in their incomes. Here is how a study published in *Health Affairs* characterizes the situation for adults with family incomes below 200 percent of the federal poverty level:[133]

> Nearly 40 percent of adults experienced a disruption in Medicaid eligibility within the first six months. After a year, 38 percent were no longer eligible, and an additional 16 percent had lost eligibility

but then regained it (churning). By three years, 47 percent of adults had incomes above the 133 percent cutoff, and an additional 30 percent of adults were below the cutoff but had experienced at least one episode of churning. By the end of the study period at four years, only 19 percent of adults would have been continuously eligible for Medicaid.

All of these problems have one and only one source: The federal government is giving markedly different subsidies to people at the same income level, depending on where they get their insurance. With a universal tax credit that is independent of income, it would not matter where people get their insurance. If everyone could be in Medicaid, regardless of income, Medicaid enrollees could stay there if they like. If everyone in Medicaid could claim the tax credit and buy private insurance, they could keep their insurance regardless of fluctuations in income.

This change would work best if the universal tax credit were set at the level the Congressional Budget Office estimates a new enrollee in Medicaid will cost. Currently, that's about $2,500 for an adult and $8,000 for a family of four.

The Financial Burden of High Deductibles Would Be Reduced

The out-of-pocket exposure for plans in the health insurance exchanges can be as high as $6,600 for individuals and $13,200 for families in 2015. And this is only for in-network expenses. If a patient has to go out of network to get needed care or a lifesaving drug, the insurer may pay nothing.

To reduce this burden and the horror stories it is likely to produce,[134] we should spend fewer taxpayer dollars subsidizing benefits people may not want or need and use the savings to match contributions to Roth Health Saving Accounts. For example, we might match the first $1,000 contributed for an adult and the first $500 for a child. The deposit could be made by the enrollee, the insurer, or an employer. With this opportunity in place, insurers would almost certainly offer plans with $1,000 HSA deposits because they could use the government's $1,000 match to make their total package more attractive.

There Would Be Real Protection for Pre-existing Conditions

Just like the Medicare Advantage program, in a well-run exchange, insurers should always receive premiums that are actuarially fair. That is, the insurer's premium should equal the enrollee's expected medical costs. The enrollees themselves will pay a community-rated premium. If there is an additional cost, it should be paid by the enrollee's previous insurer. Put differently, no insurance pool (whether inside or outside the exchange) should ever be able to dump its high-cost, sickest enrollees on an exchange plan. This ensures that health plans have ideal incentives to compete for all potential enrollees, regardless of health status. It also encourages health plans to become high-quality, low-cost providers of specialized care, say, for heart disease or cancer.

At the same time, individuals should not be allowed to game the system. For example, no one should be allowed to upgrade to a richer plan (with more benefits), paying a community-rated premium, after he or she develops a costly illness. After a one-time enrollment, people who wish to upgrade to a richer plan should be charged the full actuarial cost of the upgrade. If they downgrade, they should realize the full actuarial savings.

Similarly, no one should be allowed to remain uninsured until sickness arrives and then buy insurance for the same premium everyone else is paying. As in the Medicare Parts B and D programs and in the Medigap market, people should be penalized if they do not insure at the first opportunity. The ideal penalty is medical underwriting.

In a well-run insurance marketplace, people will pay the full cost and reap the full benefits of every change they make. That leaves them with an undistorted economic incentive to buy insurance and to choose the insurance that best meets their individual and family needs.

The Results

With these four changes, we will have converted a health system in which incentives are perverse in every direction into one in which everyone's economic incentives are ideal.

11

The Case for a Fixed-Sum Tax Credit

THE MOST IMPORTANT question in health reform is this: How should the government encourage the purchase of private health insurance? I believe that the encouragement should come in the form of a fixed-sum tax credit. The issue warrants special discussion.

Consider the traditional way of encouraging health insurance. For employer-provided insurance, the inducement is in the form of a tax exemption. Unlike wages, employer premium payments are not included in the employee's taxable income. For the self-employed, the inducement is in the form of a tax deduction. And for other individuals, health insurance premiums and medical expenses can be deducted to the extent that they exceed 10 percent of adjusted gross income.

In all three cases, people face the following perverse incentives:

- If they purchase more insurance, their taxes will go down, and if they purchase less health insurance, their taxes will go up. In this way, the tax system encourages all of us to choose more generous coverage than we would otherwise select.
- If we combine a 15-percent (FICA) payroll tax with a 25-percent federal income tax and a 5-percent state and local income tax, a middle-income family is facing a 45 percent marginal tax rate. In high-tax states, the rate can exceed 50 percent—even though the family is far from wealthy.

- At a 50-percent marginal tax rate, government at all levels is paying for half the cost of any additional insurance the family chooses to buy. Insurance that costs $1 will be viewed as worthwhile, even if the buyer views it as worth only 51 cents.

In other words, insurance can be extremely wasteful and still be attractive to tax-subsidized purchasers. Alternatively, if the buyer saves a dollar by choosing less generous coverage, that dollar will become taxable income. The government will seize one-half of it. This tax treatment helps explain a great deal of waste in our healthcare system.

But those incentives change significantly under a fixed-sum tax credit. Here is how it works in the ACA exchange:

$$\text{Subsidy} = \text{Premium}^*(1 - hY),$$

where Premium* is the second-lowest premium charged for Silver plans, Y is the buyer's income, and h is the maximum fraction of income people have to pay for such a plan. Notice that this sets the subsidy at a fixed-dollar amount.

The tax subsidy is refundable: Buyers get the credit even if they don't owe any income taxes. It is also advanceable: within the exchange, the subsidy goes directly to the insurer, bypassing the buyer altogether. But most important, the subsidy is the same whether the individual chooses another silver plan or a bronze, gold, or platinum plan. That means that buyers who choose more expensive plans pay 100 percent of the extra premium out of their own pockets. Alternatively, buyers who choose a less expensive bronze plan get to keep 100 percent of the savings.

Any extra expense is paid with after-tax dollars. Any reduction in expense increases the buyer's after-tax resources. Since most other consumption is also paid with after-tax dollars, this puts health insurance premiums and other goods and services on a level playing field.

With a fixed-sum tax credit, buyers are not encouraged to overinsure or underinsure. Every costly feature of health insurance (lower deductibles and copayments, wider networks, more generous benefits) will be at the expense of all other ways of spending the consumer's dollars.

If there is a fault in the ACA in this regard it is that it doesn't go far enough. The credit vanishes after family income reaches 400 percent of the federal poverty level and the traditional subsidies (described above) kick in. Also, it leaves the traditional tax treatment of employer-provided coverage fully in place.

In the 2008 election, John McCain proposed a more radical approach: a fixed-sum tax credit to replace all existing tax subsidies for health insurance.[135] The credit would be the same regardless of where the insurance is obtained—at work, in the marketplace, or in an exchange.[136] The legislative version of the McCain plan was the Coburn/Burr/Ryan/Nunes bill.[137]

Although President Obama and Democrats in Congress often say the Republicans have no alternative to the ACA, they appear to have very short memories. The Obama campaign spent millions of dollars disparaging the McCain health plan.[138] Judging by the number of Obama TV ads, it was the principal issue of the entire election. And when the ACA finally came to a vote in the Senate, Majority Leader Harry Reid refused to allow a vote on the Coburn/Burr alternative.

Other Republican approaches have not gone as far as the McCain approach, but they too adopt the fixed tax credit as the vehicle for subsidy:

The House Republican Study Committee plan (Roe bill) replaces existing tax subsidies with a uniform tax credit, but since the credit is not refundable, it provides very little benefit to the bottom half of the income distribution.

Rep. Tom Price has a bill that creates credits for those who buy their own insurance but leaves the employer-based system in place.

A new Coburn/Burr/Hatch bill, the Patient CARE Act, was introduced in January 2014.[139] It mimics the ACA approach (tax credits that phase out for the individual market but are less generous), but it limits the amount of health spending that can be excluded from income at work.

A 2017 Project proposal would make the new Coburn tax credit independent of income and would even create a special tax credit for HSAs, but it would leave the current employer system largely intact.[140]

Here's the bottom line: it is now well established in both political parties that the credit approach is better than all others. For example, prior to becoming President Obama's chairman of the Council of Economic Advisers, Jason Furman endorsed a health reform that looked very much like the John McCain proposal.[141] So in thinking about how to reform the ACA (or replace it), we all should be thinking about how to extend tax credits to everyone.

All of the approaches above are primarily focused on how to subsidize third-party insurance. But presumably, we don't want third parties (insurers, employers, and government) to pay every medical bill. Significant cost sharing means that individuals must self-insure for their portion of the costs, and one way to formally do that is through an HSA. How does that fit into the tax credit scheme?

Mark Pauly and I answered this question in an article in *Health Affairs* published in 1995.[142] Consider again how the tax credit works. Taxpayers get a dollar-for-dollar subsidy for a certain amount of health insurance. Presumably this is the core insurance that we want everyone to have. The current system subsidizes the last dollar just as much as the first dollar. The tax credit subsidizes only the first dollars. Marginal purchases are made only with unsubsidized, after-tax dollars.

So in order to put third-party insurance and individual self-insurance on a level playing field, we need deposits to HSA accounts to also be made with after-tax dollars. That means that the appropriate account must be a Roth-type account, with after-tax deposits and tax-free withdrawals.

A Roth HSA could replace the plethora of existing accounts: Regular HSAs, medical savings accounts (MSAs), health reimbursement arrangements (HRAs), and flexible spending accounts (FSAs). (See my 2012 survey article in *Health Affairs*.)[143] It should be completely flexible—wrapping around any third-party insurance plan and permitting maximum experimentation and innovation to find new and better ways of managing healthcare costs, especially the cost of chronic illness. A model to follow is Medicaid's Cash and Counseling program, which enables homebound disabled patients to manage their own budgets. (See my 2010 international survey of similar accounts in *Health Affairs*.)[144]

From their inception, many Democrats criticized HSAs, calling them a sop for the wealthy and the healthy. Yet Senator Jay Rockefeller was one of a number of Democrats who greatly admired the Cash and Counseling program. Given this history, perhaps we should engage in some relabeling. To achieve bipartisan harmony, we might consider calling the Roth HSA accounts "Rockefeller Accounts."

12

Why I Am More Egalitarian on Healthcare Than Most Liberals

MOST PEOPLE WOULD place me on the political right. Yet when it comes to healthcare, I am more egalitarian than almost everybody on the left.

To introduce the discussion, I need to make three distinctions. First, almost everybody on the left believes in a defined-benefit approach to healthcare. My approach centers on defined contributions. Suppose you live in Britain, and your kidneys give out. The British socialists created a National Health Service (NHS) that promises to meet all your healthcare needs, but it may not always deliver. Britain has one of the lowest dialysis rates in all of Europe.[145] In the United States, we also take a defined benefit approach to kidney care, and we actually deliver. Even if you are 80 years old and dying of cancer, you can get dialysis and maybe even a kidney transplant—all courtesy of Uncle Sam. But it would be impossible to provide all healthcare that way.

The ACA is an example of a defined-benefit approach. The law lays out in specific detail all manner of healthcare people are entitled to receive— sometimes with no deductible or copayment. But it does almost nothing to ensure that providers will actually be able to deliver what has been promised.[146] After 2018, the problem will get immeasurably worse as the ACA subsidies grow no faster than gross domestic product, while the cost of the insurance that everyone has to buy will be growing at a higher rate.

Were I designing these systems, I would give Britons and Americans a fixed sum of money (the defined contribution) and let competition in the marketplace determine what care can be insured for that sum. For example, a health plan might specify in advance that it covers kidney care for otherwise healthy people but limited care (and certainly no transplant) for someone who is terminally ill. Unlike the ACA, I would allow health plans to adopt cost-effectiveness standards, make coverage decisions based on those standards, and advertise this fact in advance of enrollment. In other words, limits on coverage would be visible and transparent—not hidden and murky.

Second, almost everybody on the left prefers rationing by waiting to rationing by price. If you make the money price zero, you guarantee that demand will exceed supply for almost every kind of care. So what determines who gets what? The knee-jerk response from people on the left is to assume that rationing by price favors the rich whereas rationing by waiting favors the poor. In fact the reverse is often true.[147] If there are long waits to see doctors, rest assured that the wealthy and the powerful will get to the head of the queue in almost every country. But walk-in clinics (with posted money prices) are potentially providing low-cost, high-quality care to low-income families in cities all across America.

Just to drive this point home, the American healthcare system today (which is not what I favor) is probably more egalitarian than the health systems of either Canada or Britain.[148]

Finally, every system in which care is rationed leaves individuals with the opportunity to pay out of pocket to obtain the care they cannot promptly get from their primary insurer. In Britain, a vibrant parallel system of private care and private health insurance exists alongside the NHS. In Canada, there are fewer private options, but Canadians can cross the U.S. border for care—and many do. Invariably, people with money who are also defenders of socialized medicine take advantage of these options—giving rise (naturally) to charges of hypocrisy.

I would incorporate out-of-pocket spending options in a much fairer and much more straightforward way. I would encourage everyone—rich and poor—to consider adding personal funds to their public subsidy in order to obtain more and prompter care. Consider the case of Britain. In 2002, the *Guardian* noted that an estimated 25,000 British cancer patients die prematurely because the NHS does not cover drugs that are routinely available in the United States and on the European continent.[149] These drugs are generally very expensive, and in most cases, they probably buy only a few months more of life. Patients who buy them privately, however, do so at considerable personal expense. I would allow supplemental insurance to cover the cost of these drugs. This insurance would likely be very inexpensive if purchased by healthy people.

More generally, I would allow people to add to their defined contribution and buy richer, more generous insurance if that is what they prefer.

In January 2013, the Obama administration announced a long list of groups whose members would be exempt from the ACA mandate to buy health insurance.[150] These included the Amish, Mennonites, legal aliens, Indian tribes, the homeless, and millions of people who are not required to file income tax returns. By contrast, I would not have any mandate, and I would not leave anybody out. I would offer the tax credit to everyone. I would also make unclaimed tax credit money available to pay for the care of any uninsured person who cannot pay his medical bills.

I would keep Medicaid as a backstop. Everyone would be permitted to add, say, about $500 to his refundable tax credit and enroll in Medicaid. By the same token, people enrolled in Medicaid would be free to leave that system and claim a tax credit to purchase private coverage if they prefer.

I would not allow anyone to game the system, however. People would not be able to wait until they get sick to buy insurance or upgrade to more generous insurance with impunity.

I would place very few restrictions on what people must buy to qualify for the tax credits, other than these two: (1) reasonable catastrophic insurance, and (2) change of health status insurance that would pay the extra premium needed if a person's health deteriorated after becoming insured and he or she needed to switch to another health plan. The first restriction protects society by insisting that people insure for care they are unlikely to be able to purchase on their own. The second leaves the insurance market free to price risk—thereby allowing a market for the care of sick people to thrive and flourish, as health plans compete to solve their problems.

Also, I would reestablish one ACA program that could be very useful: the federal risk pools. These are a much better way to deal with the problems of preexisting conditions than is the destruction of the market for risk. The risk pools should also provide coverage for changes of health status—paying the extra premium needed if a chronic patient leaves the risk pool and enters another plan in the future.

Except for temporary extra help for the chronically ill (risk pools) and what should be temporary help for the poor (Medicaid), government would essentially treat everyone the same. Everyone would be given the same basic subsidy. Individual choice and the marketplace would otherwise be free to solve the remaining problems.

The result would be a healthcare system that would be unquestionably more equitable than what you see in either Britain or Canada and a lot more equitable than what we will experience under the ACA.

Notes

1. Liz Hamel, Jamie Firth, and Mollyann Brodie, "Kaiser Health Tracking Poll: March 2014," Henry J. Kaiser Family Foundation, March 26, 2014, http://kff.org /health-reform/poll-finding/kaiser-health-tracking-poll-march-2014/.

2. Marguerite Bowling, "Video of the Week: 'We Have to Pass the Bill so You Can Find Out What Is In It,'" Heritage Foundation, *The Daily Signal,* March 10, 2010, http://dailysignal.com/2010/03/10/video-of-the-week-we-have-to-pass-the-bill-so -you-can-find-out-what-is-in-it/.

3. Christian Hagist and Laurence J. Kotlikoff, "Health Care Spending: What the Future Will Look Like," NCPA Policy Report No. 286, June 2006, http://www .ncpa.org/pdfs/st286.pdf.

4. Robert J. Samuelson, "The Health Spending Mystery," *The Washington Post*, August 7, 2013, http://www.washingtonpost.com/opinions/robert-samuelson-the-health -spending-mystery/2013/08/07/53f036a2-ff77-11e2-96a8-d3b921c0924a_story.html.

5. G. F. Anderson, B. K. Frogner, and U. E. Reinhardt, "Health Spending in OECD Countries in 2004: An Update," *Health Affairs* 26, no. 5 (2007): 1481–89; Gerard F. Anderson, et al., "Health Spending and Outcomes: Trends in OECD Countries, 1960–1998," *Health Affairs* 19, no. 3 (2000): 150–57.

6. Gina Kolata, "Vast Study Casts Doubts on Value of Mammograms," *New York Times,* February 11, 2014, http://www.nytimes.com/2014/02/12/health/study-adds -new-doubts-about-value-of-mammograms.html?_r=2.

7. John Goodman, "Bizarre Obamacare Incentives," National Center for Policy Analysis, *Health Policy Blog,* May 1, 2014, http://healthblog.ncpa.org/bizarre-obamacare -incentives/.

8. Larry Wedekind, "Power to the Physicians, Not the Hospitals," National Center for Policy Analysis, *Health Policy Blog,* June 6, 2012, http://healthblog.ncpa.org /power-to-the-physicians-not-the-hospitals/.

9. Public letter from Douglas W. Elmendorf, Director of the Congressional Budget Office, to Speaker of the House John Boehner, July 24, 2012, http://cbo.gov/sites /default/files/cbofiles/attachments/43471-hr6079.pdf. See also The Boards of Trustees, Federal Hospital Insurance and Federal Supplementary Medical Insurance

Trust Funds, *The 2013 Annual Report of the Boards of Trustees of the Federal Hospital Insurance and Federal Supplementary Medical Insurance Trust Funds.* Centers for Medicare & Medicaid Services, 13: Table II.C1.—Ultimate Assuptions (Washington, DC, May 31, 2013), http://www.cms.gov/Research-Statistics-Data-and-Systems/Statistics-Trends-and-Reports/ReportsTrustFunds/Trustees-Reports-Items/2012-2014.html?DLPage=1&DLSort=0&DLSortDir=descending.

10. Marilyn Werber Serafini, "FAQ: How Paul Ryan Proposes to Change Medicare," *Kaiser Health News*, August 11, 2012, http://www.kaiserhealthnews.org/stories/2012/august/11/faq-paul-ryan-house-republican-medicare-plan.aspx.

11. John Goodman, "What's Wrong with the Health Care Media," National Center for Policy Analysis, *Health Policy Blog,* July 18, 2012, http://healthblog.ncpa.org/whats-wrong-with-the-health-care-media/.

12. "Medicare Payments to Physicians (Updated)," *Health Policy Briefs* 33 (2014), http://www.healthaffairs.org/healthpolicybriefs/brief.php?brief_id=83.

13. Goodman, "What's Wrong."

14. John D. Shatto and M. Kent Clemens, "Projected Medicare Expenditures under Illustrative Scenarios with Alternative Payment Updates to Medicare Providers," Centers for Medicare & Medicaid Services, Department of Health and Human Services, May 18, 2012, http://www.cms.gov/Research-Statistics-Data-and-Systems/Statistics-Trends-and-Reports/ReportsTrustFunds/Downloads/2012TRAlternativeScenario.pdf.

15. Jack Hadley and John Holahan, "Covering the Uninsured: How Much Would It Cost?" *Health Affairs* Web Exclusive, June 4, 2003, http://content.healthaffairs.org/content/early/2003/06/04/hlthaff.w3.250.pdf.

16. *Preventive Care Benefits,* HealthCare.gov, https://www.healthcare.gov/what-are-my-preventive-care-benefits/#part=1.

17. John Goodman, "Could Wasteful Healthcare Spending Be Good for the Economy?" *The Health Care Blog,* January 31, 2013, http://thehealthcareblog.com/blog/tag/medicare-wellness-exams/.

18. Damon Adams, "Who Has 7-Plus Hours a Day to Put Toward Preventive Care?" *American Medical News*, April 21, 2003, http://www.ama-assn.org/amednews/2003/04/21/prsc0421.htm.

19. David P. Sklar, MD, "How Many Doctors Will We Need? A Special Issue on the Physician Workforce," *Academic Medicine* 88, no. 12 (2013): 1785–1787. doi: 10.1097 ACM.0000000000000030.

20. Louise B. Russell, "Preventing Chronic Disease: An Important Investment, but Don't Count on Cost Savings," *Health Affairs* 28 (2009): 42–45. doi: 10.1377/hlthaff.28.1.42.

21. John Goodman, "Concierge Medicine Taking Off," National Center for Policy Analysis, *Health Policy Blog,* February 8, 2013, http://healthblog.ncpa.org/concierge-medicine-taking-off/.

22. John C. Goodman, "For the Vulnerable, Expect Less Access to Care," National Center for Health Policy Analysis, *Health Policy Blog,* November 16, 2011, http://healthblog.ncpa.org/for-the-vulnerable-expect-less-access-to-care/.

23. Katherine Baicker et al., for the Oregon Health Study Group, "The Oregon Experiment—Effects of Medicaid on Clinical Outcomes," *New England Journal of Medicine* 368 (2013): 1713–22, http://www.nejm.org/doi/full/10.1056/NEJMsa1212321.

24. Congressional Budget Office, "Effects of the Affordable Care Act on Health Insurance Coverage—Baseline Projections," April 14, 2014, http://www.cbo.gov/publication/43900.

25. Gregory W. Sullivan, "Report Pursuant to Section 156 of Chapter 68 of the Acts of 2011: Rates of Reimbursement to Providers in the MassHealth MCO Program," Office of the Inspector General Commonwealth of Massachusetts, July 2012, http://www.mass.gov/ig/publications/reports-and-recommendations/2012/rates-of-reimbursement-masshealth-mco-providers-july-2012.pdf.

26. Aaron Carroll and Austin Frakt, "Oregon Medicaid—Power Problems Are Important," *The Incidental Economist* (blog), May 3, 2013, http://theincidentaleconomist.com/wordpress/oregon-medicaid-power-problems-are-important/.

27. "The Oregon Trial," *Wall Street Journal,* May 2, 2013, http://online.wsj.com/news/articles/SB10001424127887323362800457845745319436508.

28. Brent R. Asplin et al., "Insurance Status and Access to Urgent Ambulatory Care Follow-up Appointments," *The Journal of the American Medical Association* 294 (2005): 1248–54, http://jama.jamanetwork.com/article.aspx?articleid=201518.

29. John Goodman, "Is Medicaid Real Insurance?" National Center for Policy Analysis, *Health Policy Blog,* March 30, 2011, http://healthblog.ncpa.org/is-medicaid-real-insurance/.

30. Austin Frakt, "Comparing the Massachusetts Mortality Study to the Oregon Medicaid Study," *The Incidental Economist* (blog), May 7, 2014, http://theincidentaleconomist.com/wordpress/comparing-the-massachusetts-mortality-study-to-the-oregon-medicaid-study/.

31. Tom Daschle, Jeanne M. Lambrew, and Scott S. Greenberger, *Critical: What We Can Do About the Health-Care Crisis.* New York: Thomas Dunne Books, 2008.

32. Chris Conover, What Safer Cars Tell Us about Obamacare," *Forbes,* December 22, 2014, http://www.forbes.com/sites/theapothecary/2014/12/22/what-safer-cars-tell-us-about-obamacare/.

33. John Goodman and Devon Herrick, "Why Perry Made the Right Call on Medicaid," *Dallas News,* July 25, 2012, http://www.dallasnews.com/opinion/latest-columns/20120725-john-goodman-and-devon-herrick-why-perry-made-the-right-call-on-medicaid.ece.

34. John Goodman, et al., *Handbook on State Health Care Reform.* Dallas: National Center for Policy Analysis, 2007, http://www.ncpa.org/email/State_HC_Reform_6-8-07.pdf.

35. Benjamin D. Sommers, MD, PhD, and Arnold M. Epstein, MD, "Medicaid Expansion—The Soft Underbelly of Health Care Reform?" *New England Journal of Medicine* 363 (Nov. 25, 2010): 2085–87, doi: 10.1056/NEJMp1010866.

36. Avik Roy, "Oregon Study: Medicaid 'Had No Significant Effect' on Health Outcomes vs. Being Uninsured," *Forbes, The Apothecary* (blog), May 2, 2013, http://

www.forbes.com/sites/theapothecary/2013/05/02/oregon-study-medicaid-had-no
-significant-effect-on-health-outcomes-vs-being-uninsured/.

37. Merritt Hawkins & Associates, "2009 Survey of Physician Appointment Wait
Times," 2009, http://www.merritthawkins.com/pdf/mha2009waittimesurvey.pdf.

38. "Universal Healthcare on the Rise in Latin America," The World Bank, February 14, 2013, http://www.worldbank.org/en/news/feature/2013/02/14/universal
-healthcare-latin-america.

39. Jonathan Kolstad, Mark Pauly, and Robert Town, "Little Firms, Big Mistakes: How
Should Small Employers Respond to Health Reform?" *Forbes, Tech* (blog), January 7, 2013, http://www.forbes.com/sites/wharton/2013/01/07/wharton-professors
-on-new-healthcare-requirements-impact-of-small-business-hiring/.

40. Christopher Matthews, "Why Temp Agencies Are Learning to Love the Affordable
Care Act," *Time*, June 27, 2013, http://business.time.com/2013/06/27/how-temp
-agencies-learned-to-love-the-affordable-care-act/.

41. Hancock, Jay. "Flaw in Federal Software Lets Employers Offer Plans Without Hospital Benefits, Consultants Say," *Kaiser Health News*, September 12, 2014. http://www
.kaiserhealthnews.org/Stories/2014/September/12/Flaw-In-Federal-Software-Lets
-Employers-Offer-Plans-Without-Hospital-Benefits-Consultants-Say.aspx?utm
_campaign=KHN%3A+Daily+Health+Policy+Report&utm_source=hs_email
&utm_medium=email&utm_content=14118886&_hsenc=p2ANqtz-_HZB5iW
HuaJCENZz-6C3-uGoHtk8cuSZVlUEjCgIxTIUcn77ACoL9oszU6no7Iktoo8a
fBxteY8WvshVY2ZwtUDocQHw&_hsmi=14118886

42. Federal Reserve Bank of Philadelphia, "August 2014 Business Outlook Survey," August 2014, http://www.philadelphiafed.org/research-and-data/regional-economy
/business-outlook-survey/2014/bos0814.cfm#sp.

43. John R. Graham, "New York Employers: Health Costs Up 10 Percent Next Year,
Obamacare to Blame," National Center for Policy Analysis, *Health Policy Blog*,
August 21, 2014, http://healthblog.ncpa.org/new-york-employers-health-costs-up
-10-percent-next-year-obamacare-to-blame/#sthash.BQZ4pOaZ.dpuf.

44. "Unemployed by ObamaCare: Three New Fed Surveys Highlight Damage to
Labor Market," *Wall Street Journal*, Aug. 21, 2014, http://online.wsj.com/articles
/unemployed-by-obamacare-1408664211.

45. Graham, "New York Employers."

46. David M. Cutler, "Testimony of David M. Cutler before the Committee on Energy
and Commerce, U.S. House of Representatives," March 30, 2011, http://democrats
.energycommercehouse.gov/sites/default/files/image_uploads/Testimony-David
Cutler 3-30-11.pdf.

47. "Reality-Based Economists' Letter on the Affordable Care Act," January 26, 2011,
http://delong.typepad.com/sdj/2011/01/sensible-economists-letter-on-the-affordable
-care-act.html.

48. Casey B. Mulligan, "Health Care Inflation and the Arithmetic of Labor Taxes,"
Economix (blog), August 7, 2013, http://economix.blogs.nytimes.com/2013/08/07
/health-care-inflation-and-the-arithmetic-of-labor-taxes/?_php=true&_type=blogs
&emc=edit_tnt_20130807&_r=0.

49. Mulligan, "Health Care Inflation."

50. David M. Cutler, "The Economics of the Affordable Care Act," *Economix* (blog), August 7, 2013, http://economix.blogs.nytimes.com/2013/08/07/the-economics -of-the-affordable-care-act/?_r=0.

51. John Goodman, "Out-of-Pocket Costs in the California Exchange," National Center for Policy Analysis, *Health Policy Blog,* September 23, 2013, http://health blog.ncpa.org/out-of-pocket-costs-in-the-california-exchange/.

52. Available at http://www.ncpa.org/pdfs/04-130_23_Ch_22.pdf.

53. John Goodman, "How the Left and the Right View the Race to the Bottom," National Center for Policy Analysis, *Health Policy Blog,* Sept. 23, 2013, http:// healthblog.ncpa.org/how-the-left-and-the-right-view-the-race-to-the-bottom/.

54. John Goodman, "Study Devastating for Obamacare Backers," *Townhall.com*, May 4, 2013, http://townhall.com/columnists/johncgoodman/2013/05/04/study -devastating-for-obamacare-backers-n1586429/page/full.

55. "Daily Briefing by the Press Secretary Jay Carney, 09/25/13," The White House Office of the Press Secretary, September 25, 2013, http://www.whitehouse.gov/the -press-office/2013/09/25/daily-briefing-press-secretary-jay-carney-092513.

56. David Maly, "Texas Prepares to Shutter High-Risk Insurance Pool," *Texas Tribune,* October 17, 2013, http://www.texastribune.org/2013/10/17/texas-prepares-shutter -high-risk-insurance-pool/.

57. "Coverage of Uninsurable Pre-existing Conditions: State and Federal High-Risk Pools," National Conference of State Legislatures, http://www.ncsl.org/research /health/high-risk-pools-for-health-coverage.aspx.

58. Hadley Heath and Heather Higgins, "ObamaCare's Preexisting Problems Need a Pragmatic Fix," *The Hill* (blog), April 23, 2013, http://thehill.com/blogs/congress -blog/healthcare/295587-obamacares-preexisting-problems-need-a-pragmatic-fix.

59. John Goodman, "Detroit Is Trying to Dump Its Retirees on the Exchange," National Center for Policy Analysis, *Health Policy Blog,* October 18, 2013, http://health blog.ncpa.org/detroit-is-trying-to-dump-its-retirees-on-the-exchange/.

60. Michael Meulemans, "10% of Large Employers May Drop 2014 Health Benefits," *About.com Insurance* (blog), http://insurance.about.com/od/HealthIns/a/In-2014 -Ten-Percent-of-large-Employers-May-Cease-Health-Benefits.htm.

61. John Goodman, "Rational Health Insurance," National Center for Policy Analysis, *Health Policy Blog,* Apr. 10, 2009, http://healthblog.ncpa.org/rational-health -insurance/.

62. Uwe E. Reinhardt, Peter S. Hussey, and Gerard F. Anderson, "US Healthcare Spending in an International Context," *Health Affairs* 23, No. 3 (May 2004): 10–25.

63. "On Average, Patients Pay Only 12 Percent of Medical Care Out of Pocket." Centers for Medicare and Medicaid Services, U.S. Department of Health and Human Services, *National Health Expenditures by Type of Service and Source of Funds: Calendar Years 1960 to 2009,* January 4, 2011, https://www.cms.gov/NationalHealthExpend Data/downloads/nhe2009.zip.

64. U.S. Centers for Medicare and Medicaid Services, "Preventive Health Services for Adults," https://www.healthcare.gov/what-are-my-preventive-care-benefits/.

65. Gail A. Jensen and Michael A. Morrisey, "Employer-Sponsored Health Insurance and Mandated Benefit Laws," *Milbank Quarterly* 77, no. 4 (1999), http://www .milbank.org/uploads/documents/featured-articles/html/Milbank_Quarterly_Vol -77_No-4_1999.htm.

66. Many people will opt for more comprehensive plans. See Douglas W. Elmendorf, Congressional Budget Office, "Letter to Honorable Olympia Snowe," January 11, 2010, http://www.cbo.gov/ftpdocs/108xx/doc10884/01-11-Premiums_for_Bronze _Plan.pdf.

67. Katherine Baicker and Helen Levy, "Employer Health Insurance Mandates and the Risk of Unemployment," *Risk Management and Insurance Review* 11 (2008): 109–132. doi: 10.1111/j.1540-6296.2008.00133.x.

68. Stephanie Armour, "Fewer Uninsured Face Fines as Health Law's Exemptions Swell: Almost 90% of Uninsured Won't Pay Penalty Under the Affordable Care Act in 2016," *Wall Street Journal,* Aug. 6, 2014, http://online.wsj.com/articles/fewer -uninsured-face-fines-as-health-laws-exemptions-swell-1407378602?mod=WSJ _hp_RightTopStories.

69. David Auerbach et al., "Will Health Insurance Mandates Increase Coverage? Synthesizing Perspectives from the Literature in Health Economics, Tax Compliance, and Behavioral Economics" (Working Paper 2010-05, Congressional Budget Office, August 2010), http://www.cbo.gov/sites/default/files/cbofiles/ftpdocs/116xx /doc11634/working_paper_2010-05-health_insurance_mandate.pdf.

70. John Goodman, "How to Become Exempt from the Obama-Care Mandate," National Center for Policy Analysis, *Health Policy Blog,* July 2, 2013, http://healthblog .ncpa.org/how-to-becom-exempt-from-the-obamacare-mandate/.

71. Armour, "Fewer Uninsured."

72. John C. Goodman, "Will You Be Able to Keep Your Current Health Insurance?" the Independent Institute, *The Beacon* (blog), January 30, 2013, http://blog.inde-pendent.org/2013/01/30/will-you-be-able-to-keep-your-current-health-insurance/.

73. Lisa Meyer and Hannah Rappleye, "Obama Admin. Knew Millions Could Not Keep Their Health Insurance," NBC News.com, October 28, 2013, http://www .nbcnews.com/news/other/obama-admin-knew-millions-could-not-keep-their -health-insurance-f8C11484394.

74. J. K. Wall, "Small Employers Dumping Plans Faster Than Expected, WellPoint Says," *Indiana Business Journal* (blog), August 4, 2014, http://www.ibj.com/the -dose-2014-08-04-small-employers-dumping-plans-faster-than-expected-wellpoint -says/PARAMS/post/48889.

75. Victoria C. Bunce and J. P. Wieske, *Health Insurance Mandates in the States, 2010,* Council for Affordable Health Insurance, http://www.cahi.org/cahi_contents /resources/pdf/MandatesintheStates2010.pdf.

76. John C. Goodman and Gerald L. Musgrave, *Freedom of Choice in Health Insurance,* National Center for Policy Analysis, Policy Report No. 134, 1988; Gail A. Jensen and Michael A. Morrisey, *Mandated Benefit Laws and Employer-Sponsored Health Insurance,* Health Insurance Association of America, January 25, 1999; and Stephen T. Parente et al., *Consumer Response to a National Marketplace for Individual*

Insurance, Office of the Assistant Secretary for Planning and Evaluation, U.S. Department of Health and Human Services, Final Report, June 28, 2008, http:// aspe.hhs.gov/health/reports/08/consumerresponse/report.html.

77. Personal correspondence from John Sheils of the Lewin Group. The Lewin Group estimates that in 2011 the federal tax expenditure for employee health coverage was about $274 billion annually.

78. Personal correspondence from John Sheils of the LewinGroup. For a discussion, also see John Sheils and Randall Haught, "The Cost of Tax-Exempt Health Benefits in 2004," *Health Affairs,* Web Exclusive W4 (2004): 106–12, doi: 10.1377/hlthaff .w4.106.

79. John C. Goodman, "S-CHIP Fiasco," National Center for Policy Analysis, *Health Policy Blog,* October 15, 2007, http://healthblog.ncpa.org/s-chip-fiasco/.

80. David Cutler and Jonathan Gruber, "Does Public Insurance Crowd Out Private Insurance?" *Quarterly Journal of Economics* 111, No. 2 (1996): 391–430.

81. Jonathan Gruber and Kosali Simon, *Crowd-Out Ten Years Later: Have Recent Public Insurance Expansions Crowded Out Private Health Insurance?* (Working Paper No. 12858, National Bureau of Economic Research, 2007).

82. Terry Neese and John C. Goodman, *Five Family Friendly Policies,* National Center for Policy Analysis, Brief Analysis No. 620, July 2008.

83. Emmett B. Keeler, Joseph P. Newhouse, and Robert H. Brook, "Selective Memories for 25 Years, the RAND Health Insurance Experiment Has Stoked Competing Claims," *RAND Review* 31 (2007): 26–29.

84. See Andrew J. Rettenmaier and Thomas R. Saving, *A Medicare Reform Proposal Everyone Can Love: Finding Common Ground among Medicare Reformers,* National Center for Policy Analysis, Policy Report No. 306, December 2007, http://www .ncpa.org/pub/st306; Robin Hanson, "RAND Health Insurance Experiment," *Overcoming Bias* (blog), May 8, 2007, http://www.overcomingbias.com/2007/05 /rand_health_ins.html.

85. Thomas A. Massaro and Yu-Ning Wong, *Medical Savings Accounts: The Singapore Experience,* National Center for Policy Analysis, Policy Report No. 203, April 1996, http://www.ncpa.org/pub/st203.

86. Shaun Matisonn, *Medical Savings Accounts in South Africa,* National Center for Policy Analysis, Policy Report No. 234, June 2000, http://www.ncpa.org/pub /st234.

87. Greg Scandlen, *Medical Savings Accounts: Obstacles to Their Growth and Ways to Improve Them,* National Center for Policy Analysis, Policy Report No. 216, July 1998.

88. John C. Goodman, *Health Savings Accounts Will Revolutionize American Health-care,* National Center for Policy Analysis, Policy Report No. 464, January 2004, http://www.ncpa.org/pub/ba464/.

89. Devon Herrick, *Health Reimbursement Arrangements: Making a Good Deal Better,* National Center for Policy Analysis, Policy Report No. 438, May 2003, http://www .ncpa.org/pub/ba438.

90. Robert Wood Johnson Foundation, *Choosing Independence: An Overview of the Cash & Counseling Model of Self-Directed Personal Assistance Services,* 2006.

91. Amelia M. Haviland, Neeraj Sood, Roland McDevitt, and Susan Marquis, "How Do Consumer-Directed Health Plans Affect Vulnerable Populations?" *Forum for Health Economics & Policy* 14, no. 2 (2011): 1–12. doi: 10.2202/1558-9544.1248.

92. Haviland et al., "How Do Consumer-Directed."

93. Haviland et al., "How Do Consumer-Directed."

94. Devon M. Herrick, *Why Health Costs Are Still Rising,* National Center for Policy Analysis, Brief Analysis No. 731, November 2010.

95. "LASIK Lessons," *Wall Street Journal,* March 10, 2006, A18. Also see Ha T. Tu and Jessica H. May, "Self-Pay Markets in Health Care: Consumer Nirvana or Caveat Emptor?" *Health Affairs* 26, No. 2 (2007): w217–w226. doi: 10.1377/hlthaff .26.2.w217.

96. Devon M. Herrick, *Consumer Driven Healthcare: The Changing Role of the Patient,* National Center for Policy Analysis, Policy Report No. 276, May 2005.

97. Herrick, *Consumer Driven Healthcare.*

98. Devon M. Herrick, *Shopping for Drugs: 2007,* National Center for Policy Analysis, Policy Report No. 293, November 2006.

99. Herrick, *Shopping for Drugs: 2007.*

100. Devon M. Herrick, *Retail Clinics: Convenient and Affordable Care,* National Center for Policy Analysis, Brief Analysis No. 686, January 2010.

101. Minnesota HealthScores website, http://www.mnhealthcare.org/.

102. Devon M. Herrick, *Convenient Care and Telemedicine,* National Center for Policy Analysis, Brief Analysis No. 305, November 2007.

103. Devon M. Herrick, *Concierge Medicine: Convenient and Affordable Care,* National Center for Policy Analysis, Brief Analysis No. 687, January 2010.

104. Herrick, *Concierge Medicine.*

105. "Dallas-based Compass Turns Patients into Smart Consumers," *Dallas Morning News,* September 10, 2011.

106. Mark V. Pauly and John C. Goodman, "Tax Credits for Health Insurance and Medical Savings Accounts," *Health Affairs* 14 (1995): 125–39.

107. John C. Goodman, *The John McCain Health Plan,* National Center for Policy Analysis, Brief Analysis No. 629, September 5, 2008, http://www.ncpa.org/pub /ba629/.

108. Tom Coburn et al., *The Impact of the 2009 The Patient's Choice Act,* HIS Network, LLC, independent assessment, http://www.hsinetwork.com/HSI_Report _on _PCHOICE_07-21-2009.pdf.

109. The law requires an across-the-board deductible for all covered services with the exception of preventive care.

110. Matisonn, *Medical Savings Accounts in South Africa.*

111. Of course, without some oversight, this reimbursement formula encourages discretionary procedures to relocate to a hospital setting.

112. Shaun Matisonn, *Medical Savings Accounts and Prescription Drugs: Evidence from South Africa,* National Center for Policy Analysis, Policy Report No. 254, August 2002.

113. A mandatory point of service option when combined with a requirement to reimburse at the same rates in and out of network can raise the cost of health insurance by as much as 11.3 percent. Estimates of M&R for the National Center for Policy Analysis. Cited in Merrill Matthews, *Can We Afford Consumer Protection? An Analysis of the PARCA Bill,* National Center for Policy Analysis, Brief Analysis No. 249, November 24, 1997.

114. Niteesh K. Choudhry, Meredith B. Rosenthal, and Arnold Milstein, "Assessing the Evidence for Value-Based Insurance Design," *Health Affairs* 29 (2010): 1988–94.

115. "From Reference Pricing to Value Pricing," Catalyst for Payment Reform, http://www.catalyzepaymentreform.org/images/documents/CPR_Action_Brief_Reference_Pricing.pdf.

116. See A. Faas, F. G. Schellevis, and J. T. Van Eijk, "The Efficacy of Self-Monitoring of Blood Glucose in NIDDM Subjects: A Criteria-Based Literature Review," *Diabetes Care* 20, no. 9 (1997): 1482–86, doi: 10.2337/diacare.20.9.1482.

117. Matisonn, *Medical Savings Accounts in South* Africa; Matisonn, *Medical Savings Accounts and Prescription Drugs.*

118. James C. Robinson and Timothy T. Brown, "Changes in Patient Volumes, Allowed Charges, Consumer Cost Sharing, and CalPERS Payments for Orthopedic Surgery Associated with Reference Pricing," Berkeley Center for Health Technology, University of California, Berkeley, http://www.calpers.ca.gov/eip-docs/about/committee-meetings/agendas/pension/201306/item-7-attach-1.pdf.

119. See John C. Goodman, *Regulation of Medical Care: Is the Price Too High?* (Cato Institute Public Policy Research Monograph), 1980.

120. Although for the terminally ill, this is an idea worth considering.

121. Jensen and Morrisey, *Mandated Benefit Laws.*

122. There is a growing literature on how to design such arrangements. See John H. Cochrane, "Time-Consistent Health Insurance," *Journal of Political Economy* 103 (1995): 445–73; Mark V. Pauly, Howard Kunreuther, and Richard Hirth, "Guaranteed Renewability in Insurance," *Journal of Risk and Uncertainty* 10 (1995): 143–56. See also Bradley Herrick and Mark Pauly, *Incentive-Compatible Guaranteed Renewable Health Insurance* (Working Paper 9888, National Bureau of Economic Research, July 2003); and Vip Patel and Mark V. Pauly, "Guaranteed Renewability and the Problem of Risk Variation in Individual Health Insurance Markets," *Health Affairs* Web exclusive (August 28, 2002), http://news.ehealthinsurance.com/_ir/68/20125/Vips_HealthAffairs_RenewabilitySept-Oct02.pdf.

123. What is envisioned here is a market for individual patients. For those who doubt that such a market could develop, recall that the same objection was once raised against a reinsurance market for residential housing.

124. Linda J. Blumberg, John Holahan, and Matthew Buettgens, "Why Not Just Eliminate the Employer Mandate?" Robert Wood Johnson Foundation, Urban Institute, May 2014, http://www.rwjf.org/content/dam/farm/reports/issue_briefs/2014

/rwjf413248; John Goodman, "Is ObamaCare Causing the Jobless Recovery?" National Center for Policy Analysis, *Health Policy Blog,* July 16, 2012, http://health blog.ncpa.org/is-obamacare-causing-the-jobless-recovery/.

125. Armour, "Fewer Uninsured."

126. Congressional Budget Office, "Insurance Coverage Provisions of the Affordable Care Act—CBO's February 2014 Baseline," http://www.cbo.gov/sites/default/files /cbofiles/attachments/43900-2014-02-ACAtables.pdf.

127. Goodman, "How the Left."

128. Goodman, "Rational Health."

129. John Goodman, "You Can't Buy Insurance until Next November," National Center for Policy Analysis, *Health Policy Blog,* Apr. 7, 2014, http://healthblog.ncpa.org /you-cant-buy-insurance-until-next-november/.

130. Goodman, "How the Left."

131. David Blumenthal, MD, "Reflecting on Health Reform—Narrow Networks: Boon or Bane?" *The Commonwealth Fund Blog,* February 24, 2014, http://www.common wealthfund.org/publications/blog/2014/feb/narrows-networks-boon-or-bane.

132. Goodman, "Rational Health."

133. Benjamin D. Sommers and Sara Rosenbaum, "Issues in Health Reform: How Changes in Eligibility May Move Millions Back and Forth Between Medicaid and Insurance Exchanges," *Health Affairs* 30 (2011): 228–36, http://content.healthaffairs .org/content/30/2/228.full.

134. See., e.,g., "Edie Sundby's Choice," *Wall Street Journal,* November 7, 2013, http:// online.wsj.com/news/articles/SB10001424052702303936904579177930307493584.

135. John Goodman, "McCain Is the Radical on Health Reform," *Wall Street Journal,* July 30, 2008, http://online.wsj.com/news/articles/SB121737388416495023.

136. Robert E. Moffit, Ph.D., and Nina Owcharenko, "The McCain Health Care Plan: More Power to Families," Backgrounder #2198, Heritage Foundation, October 15, 2008, http://www.heritage.org/research/reports/2008/10/the-mccain-health-care -plan-more-power-to-families.

137. Tom Coburn, MD, "Health Care," http://www.coburnsenate.gov/public/?p =Healthcare.

138. Jim Rutenberg, "Nearing Record, Obama's Ad Effort Swamps McCain," *New York Times,* October 17, 2008, http://www.nytimes.com/2008/10/18/us/politics/18ads .htm.

139. "Dr. Coburn Unveils Obamacare Replacement—Patient CARE Act—with Senators Burr and Hatch" (Press Release), January 27, 2014, http://www.coburn.senate. gov/public/index.cfm/pressreleases?ContentRecord_id=bd2f1e3a-3c25-4ea2-80a0 -25b0753cc6a

140. William Kristol and Jeffrey H. Anderson, "A Winning Alternative to Obamacare," *The Blog,* February 10, 2014, http://www.weeklystandard.com/blogs/winning -alternative-obamacare_778872.html?page=1.

141. Jason Furman, "Reforming the Tax Treatment of Health Care: Right Ways and Wrong Ways" (Preliminary Draft, The Brookings Institute, February 24, 2008),

http://www.taxpolicycenter.org/tpccontent/healthconference_furman.pdf; John Goodman, "The John McCain Health Plan," National Center for Policy Analysis, Brief Analysis 629, Sept. 5, 2008, http://www.ncpa.org/pub/ba629.

142. Mark V. Pauly and John C. Goodman, "Tax Credits for Health Insurance and Medical Savings Accounts," *Health Affairs* 14, no. 1 (1995): 125–39. http://content .healthaffairs.org/content/14/1/125.citation.

143. John Goodman, "Saving for Health Care: The Policy Pros and Cons of Different Vehicles," *Health Affairs Blog,* April 17, 2012, http://healthaffairs.org/blog/2012 /04/17/saving-for-heatlh-care-the-policy-pros-and-cons-of-different-vehicles/.

144. John Goodman, "An International Trend toward Self-Directed Care," *Health Affairs Blog,* April 9, 2010, http://healthaffairs.org/blog/2010/04/09/an-international -trend-toward-self-directed-care/.

145. OECD, "Health at a Glance 2011: Prevalence of Patients Undergoing Dialysis, 1990 and 2009 (or Nearest Year)," http://dx.doi.org/10.1787/888932524849.

146. John Goodman, "Expect Emergency Room Visits to Soar," National Center for Policy Analysis, *Health Policy Blog,* July 21, 2010, http://healthblog.ncpa.org/expect -emergency-room-visits-to-soar/.

147. John Goodman, "Everything We Are Doing in Health Policy May Be Completely Wrong," National Center for Policy Analysis, *Health Policy Blog,* July 25, 2011, http://healthblog.ncpa.org/everything-we-are-doing-in-health-policy-may-be -completely-wrong/.

148. John Goodman, "Does Socialism Work? Debunking the Myths," National Center for Policy Analysis, *Health Policy Blog,* November 26, 2007, http://healthblog .ncpa.org/does-socialism-work-debunking-the-myths/; and John C. Goodman, Gerald L. Musgrave, and Devon M. Herrick, "Equality," Chapter 2 in *Lives at Risk: Single-Payer National Health Insurance around the World* (Lanham, MD: Rowman & Littlefield, 2004), http://www.ncpa.org/pdfs/livesatrisk/Ch02.pdf.

149. "How Thousands of Cancer Patients and Doctors Have Been Betrayed," *The Guardian,* March 3, 2002, http://www.theguardian.com/society/2002/mar/03/NHS .cancercare.

150. Timothy Jost, "Implementing Health Reform: Shared Responsibility Tax Exemptions and Family Coverage Affordability," *Health Affairs Blog,* January 31, 2013, http:// healthaffairs.org/blog/2013/01/31/implementing-health-reform-shared-responsibility -tax-exemptions-and-family-coverage-affordability/.

Index

About the Author

JOHN C. GOODMAN is Senior Fellow at the Independent Institute and author of the award-winning and widely acclaimed book, *Priceless: Curing the Healthcare Crisis* from the Independent Institute. *The Wall Street Journal* and the *National Journal*, among other media, have called him the "Father of Health Savings Accounts." *Modern Healthcare* says he is one of  the four people who have most changed the modern healthcare system.

Dr. Goodman is frequently invited to testify before Congress on healthcare reform, and he is the author of more than fifty studies on health policy, retirement reform, and tax issues plus ten books, including *Living with Obamacare: A Consumer's Guide*; *Lives at Risk: Single Payer National Health Insurance Around the World* (with Gerald Musgrave and Devon Herrick); *Leaving Women Behind: Modern Families, Outdated Laws* (with Kimberley A. Strassel and Celeste Colgan); and *Patient Power: Solving America's Health Care Crisis*, which sold more than 300,000 copies. His other books include *The Handbook on State Health Care Reform*; *National*

Health Care in Great Britain: Lessons for the U.S.A.; *Economics of Public Policy: The Micro View* (with Edwin Dolan); *Fighting the War of Ideas in Latin America*; and *Privatization*.

He received his Ph.D. in economics from Columbia University and was the founder and president of the National Center for Policy Analysis. He has taught at Columbia University, Stanford University, Dartmouth College, Southern Methodist University, and the University of Dallas. In 1988, he received the prestigious Duncan Black Award for the best scholarly article in public choice economics.

Goodman regularly appears on television and radio news programs, including those on Fox News Channel, CNN, PBS, Fox Business Network and CNBC, and his articles appear in the *Wall Street Journal, Investor's Business Daily, USA Today, Forbes, National Review, Health Affairs, Kaiser Health News* and other national publications. He also directed the grassroots public policy campaign, "Free Our Health Care Now," an unsurpassed national education effort to communicate patient-centered alternatives to a government-run healthcare system. The initiative resulted in the largest online petition ever delivered on Capitol Hill.

Independent Studies in Political Economy